"Villainy and Maddness"

Washington's Flying Camp

By
Richard Lee Baker

CLEARFIELD

Published for Clearfield Company by
Genealogical Publishing Company
Baltimore, Maryland
2011

ISBN 978-0-8063-5506-1

Made in the United States of America

Table of Contents

Illustrations...

Acknowledgements

John Donne [1572-1631] provided probably the best description of the human condition when he said "No man is an island, entire of itself, every man is a piece of the continent, a part of the main." Thus, no person can solely claim to have accomplished any great single feat. No author can say they are wholly responsible for a work of minor or major magnitude. We are all a "part of the main." I'm reminded of a television documentary series called *Connections,* hosted by James Burke. As he found, I'm always being amazed by the finding of individual links that became chains binding one event distanced by time and space to another. So it is with this effort I attempt to provide a connection with those who were to "come equipped with a good Musket with a Bayonet…, a Tomahawk, a Cartouch-box, Blanket, Canteen, and Knapsack" to serve in the Flying Camp.

I'm indebted to my links from the past; parents, family, teachers, and friends. I'm honor bound and proud to salute the late Colonel (retired) John B. B. Trussell, Jr. His knowledge and sage advice on the nature of Revolutionary War units and organization was unparalleled and deeply appreciated. I also wish to laud the contributions and assistance of Dr. "Sam" Newland, formerly of the U.S. Army War College. The good doctor's wisdom and direction has served to take a fractured manuscript and weld it into a [more or less] solid presentation. To Rick Atkinson I express my sincere thanks for teaching me that history is a story, great, and never ending. His mentoring and encouragement is deeply appreciated. A heartfelt thank you goes to Colonel Robert Black, "Mr. Ranger." He has been a beacon whose generous guidance and advice has been instrumental to the telling of this story. I'm honored to have such friends as these. A particularly sincere note of admiration and appreciation is extended to my spouse, eternal partner in life, and chief editor and "mule driver" [my being the stubborn ass that needed the whip], Iris.

A greater recognition of those who strive to hold onto the history of our nation in the form of documents, photographs, and artifacts is due. This stalwart cadre provides great service and deserves the highest respect. In particular I wish to acknowledge the people of the United States Army Military History Institute in Carlisle, Pennsylvania. The stellar efforts of the staff at the United States Library of Congress to make great collections available on the web deserve special mention. The Massachusetts Historical Society elicits praise for the excellent effort to place the *Adams Family papers: An Electronic Archive* on-line. The Historical Society of Pennsylvania, Philadelphia, stands as a beacon of light shining upon rare and wonderful records of our history. The staff members of the New Jersey State Archives have proven dedicated to the cause of preserving our valuable history and deserve a sharp salute. A special accolade is reserved for one man, long gone from this world, for his valuable contributions to the preservation of our country's documentary history; Peter Force (1790-1868).

Introduction

All good research begins with a good question. A gentleman appeared at my workplace one day asking about his relative's service during the Revolutionary War. He had few details and only a minor reference to a "Flying Camp." The same subject was broached by others on several more occasions. We found only minor references to the Camp, in total being of little help. An interest developed in the subject and so I began the search for further knowledge. What I initially discovered found its way into a graduate course term paper on the American Revolution. Yet the story of the Flying Camp remained incomplete.

I've found that time has dulled the understanding of the reasons for creating the Flying Camp. Some see it as being only an effort to develop a mobile reserve of troops for General Washington's Army. A deeper examination reveals the General's far broader strategic ideas. Washington saw the force in New Jersey as an essential component in his plans for the campaigns in New York. Yet, little note has been made of his efforts and those of the Continental Congress, several State governments, and thousands of individuals to establish the Flying Camp. Mark Boatner in his *Encyclopedia of the American Revolution* refers to an "inglorious existence" and to having "some use as a source of reinforcements."[1] Other minor articles tend to reflect the roles of individual regiments and states. The best synopsis I've found is contributed by Paul J. Sanborn in *The American Revolution 1775-1783: An Encyclopedia*. He describes the Flying Camp as "What was an exciting approach on paper to a military problem was a disaster in its execution."[2] His is a thoughtful and valid appraisal, yet one I feel is still incomplete in detail and scope.

There is a need to present more of this story and the effort to create a viable American Army in 1776. I believe the best way to tell the story is in the participant's words. A treasure trove of details, letters, and documents is to be found in the series *American Archives* edited by Peter Force. It contains many true gems which provide sparkle for those reading this story.

While conducting this study I've seen distinct comparisons between the events surrounding the American Revolution and those occurring in many places today. Like many people today, our ancestors also strove to establish a new government and build a protective army. Their efforts were riddled with strife, dissention, trials and tribulations, successes and failures. The story of the Flying Camp exemplifies all of the above. It reflects the results of perseverance in the face of disaster. It provides a reminder of our own journey as a nation, composed of many minor steps forward and some major steps backwards, but always a continued march ahead into history.

---

[1] Mark Boatner. *Encyclopedia of the American Revolution*, (Mechanicsburg PA: Stackpole Books, 1994), 373.
[2] Paul J Sanborn. "Flying Camp (July –November 1776)," *The American Revolution 1775-1783 : An Encyclopedia*. Blanco, Richard L Ed.,(New York: Garland Publishing, 1993), 548-549.

Chapter 1
A Grand View

"History is a story; the greatest story"
(Rick Atkinson at USAMHI 1/7/2005)

"From Pens Hill we have a view of the largest Fleet ever seen in America. You may count upwards of 100 & 70 and Sail," wrote Abigail Adams to her husband John. "They look like a Forrest," she noted of the British fleet abandoning Boston for the open sea in March 1776.[3]   John responded to her letter on March 29th writing, "I give you joy of Boston and Charlestown, once more the Habitations of Americans."[4] The American's impressive tactical victory imposed the daunting strategic challenge of defending widely scattered areas against future invasion. This challenge would come to the forefront in early 1776, testing the resolve of the new Continental Congress and the separate State governments.

---

[3] Letter from Abigail Adams to John Adams, 16-18 march 1776 (electronic edition). *Adams Family papers: An Electronic Archive*. Massachusetts Historical Society. http://www.masshist.org/digitaladams/ .
[4] Ibid. Letter from John Adams to Abigail Adams, 29 March 1776 (electronic edition).

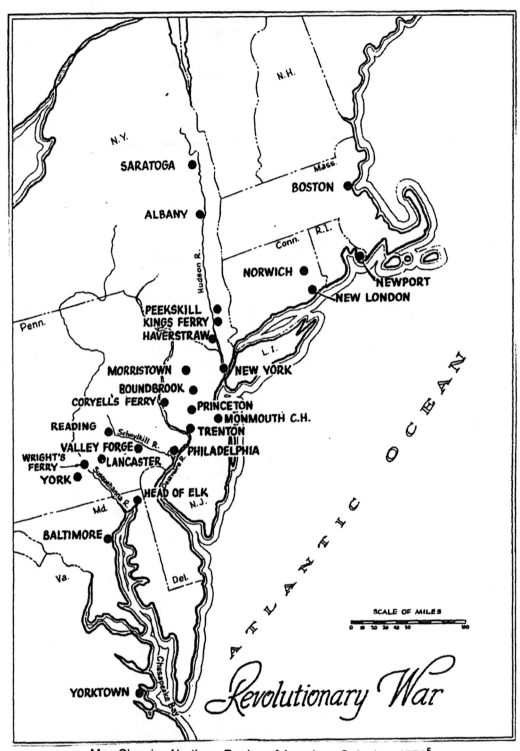

Map Showing Northern Region of American Colonies, 1776[5]

---

[5] James A. Huston. *Army History Series:* "Sinews of War: Army Logistics 1775-1953" (Washington DC: Office

8

General George Washington's strategic plans for confronting the British in 1776 included the idea of establishing a unit similar to what would today be called a rapid response force or a "mobile reserve." [6]   His ideas culminated in the creation of the Flying Camp. The term is a literal translation of *Camp Volant* (Fr). [7] Eighteenth century military terminology defines such a unit as "a strong body of horse or foot … which is always in motion to cover its own garrisons, and to keep the enemy's army in a continual alarm." [8]

In May 1776, at his headquarters in New York, General Washington felt he or his Adjutant General Horatio Gates should confer directly with Congress on issues affecting the Army. Upon further consideration he didn't feel that he should leave the city while under the threat of a British invasion. He decided to prepare General Gates to proceed to Philadelphia as his representative to Congress. The Congress, apparently of the same mind, preempted his actions when a letter from John Hancock, President of Congress, arrived at General Washington's headquarters. [9] "The Congress being of Opinion, that it is necessary, as well for your Health, as the public Service, that you should embrace the earliest opportunity of coming to Philadelphia, have directed me to write you, and request, that you will repair to Philadelphia, as soon as you can conveniently, in order to consult with Congress, upon such Measures as may be necessary for carrying on the ensuing Campaign." [10]   Thus summoned, General Washington departed New York on May 21st, arriving on the 22nd in the City of Brotherly Love.

On May 23rd with the General present, Congress "*Resolved, that a Committee of five be appointed to confer with General Washington, Major General Gates*, and Brigadier General *Mifflin* , upon the most speedy and effectual means for supporting the *American* cause in *Canada.*" [11]   Initially the committee included Benjamin Harrison and Richard Henry Lee from Virginia, John Adams of Massachusetts, James Wilson of Pennsylvania,

---

of the Chief of Military History,1966), Map 1.

[6] Freeman. *George Washington*, 103.
[7] Mark Boatner. *Encyclopedia of the American Revolution*, (Mechanicsburg PA: Stackpole Books, 1994), 371.
[8] George Smith, *A Universal Military Dictionary*, (Whitehall: J. Millan, 1779), 45.
[9] Douglas Southall Freeman. *George Washington: Leader of the Revolution*, (New York: Charles Scribner's Sons, 1948-57), 99-100.
[10]   Paul H Smith, Ed. *Letters of Delegates to Congress 1774-1789*,(Washington: Library of Congress, 1979), 8.
[11]   Peter Force, ed., ", *A Documentary History of the English Colonies in North America from the King's Message to Parliament of March 7,1774 to the Declaration of Independence of the United States.* American Archives: Fourth Series, volume VI. (Hereafter known as Force, *Archives* 4th Ser, Vol. 6)(Washington: M. St. Claire Clarke and Peter Force, 1846), Report of the Continental Congress, May 24, 1776. 1681.

9

and Edward Rutledge of South Carolina; with Robert R. Livingston of New York added on May 25th.[12] John Adams, writing on May 27th to his wife Abigail, stated "Generals Washington, Gates and Mifflin are all here and We shall derive Spirit, Unanimity, and Vigor from their Presence and Advice." [13]

On May 24th the Committee had brought forth an initial report to the Congress. The findings largely reflected General Washington's advice, though slightly modified by the members.[14] The report's main points provided little in concrete support, positive suggestions or recommended actions. The Committee of Conference was directed to "further confer" with the Generals, "touching upon the most proper Posts, and measures to be taken for effectually preventing the enemy's communication with the upper country from *Canada*, and such other measures as shall tend to secure the frontiers."[15]

On May 25th a new "Committee of Conference," was established to confer with the Generals and "concert a plan of Military operations for the ensuing campaign." All but one of the original committee members [Edward Rutledge] were appointed to this group. Along with these members new additions included Robert R Livingston (NY), William Whipple (NH), Roger Sherman (CT), Stephen Hopkins (RI), William Livingston (NJ), George Read (DE), Tench Tilghman (PA), Joseph Hewes (NC), Arthur Middleton (SC), and Lyman Hall (GA). [16]

Responding quickly to its new assignment the Committee submitted its first report that same day. Presented late in the day on Friday, some recommendations were passed as resolutions while further consideration was postponed on remaining items till the following Monday. On Saturday, May 26th, attention was focused on establishing fortifications on the St. Lawrence River to "prevent the enemy's passing to the upper country, should the forces of the *United Colonies* be forced to retreat…" Also included was a resolve "That it is highly expedient to engage the *Indians* in the service of the United Colonies." It's being the day before the Sabbath, the Congress "Adjourned to ten o'clock on *Monday.*"[17]

Congress, having previously tabled the Committee of Conference report, would not return to it until the following Wednesday, May 29th, for further deliberation. When consideration was renewed the action included the reading of the committee's further report to the assembly. Being far more detailed, this report presented essential questions for consideration and serious recommendations for action by the Congress. The report is presented herein as it is important for understanding the participant's roles and the series of events relating to the Colonial's response to British military actions. Of deeper interest is that it first reflected the idea of creating a Flying Camp.

> Report of the Committee appointed to confer with General Washington.
> The Committee appointed to confer with the Generals, &c., beg leave to report as follows:
> That it having been considered and proposed in what proportion of numbers should the enemy's force be opposed?

---

[12] George Washington. *The Writings of George Washington from the Original Manuscript Sources 1745-1799.* Ed. Fitzpatrick, John C. (Wash DC: US Government Printing Office, 1932) .Vol. 5 , 87n.
[13] Smith, *Letters of Delegates,* 80.
[14] Freeman. *George Washington,* 103.
[15] Force, *Archives* 4th Ser. Vol 6 , 1686.
[16] Ibid, Report of the Continental Congress, 1684-1685 .
[17] Ibid, 1686.

A. Two to one.

Q. What number of the enemy may it be supposed will be sent to attack Canada?

A. Ten thousand. And as the whole force at present directed for Canada, when it arrives there, will not exceed ten thousand men, therefore, upon the question, what are the proportions to be furnished by the different Provinces out of the Militia for the defence of Canada?

A. Massachusetts 4,500, Connecticut 2,000, New Hampshire 1,000, New York 1,500, Indians 1,000; total 10,000.

Q. What number of the enemy may it be supposed will attack New York?

A. Twelve thousand five hundred. And as the Continental force now at New York for the defence of that place, and the communication with Albany, does not exceed ten thousand men, therefore, upon the question, What are the proportions to be furnished by the different Provinces out of the Militia for the defence of New York, &c.?

A. Massachusetts 2,000, Connecticut 5,500, New York 3,000, New Jersey 3,300, two Battalions Pennsylvania establishment 1,200; total 15,000.

Q. What force is necessary for protection of the four New England Provinces?

A. The eleven Regiments raised and ordered to be raised in those Colonies are, in the opinion of the Committee, sufficient.

Q. Should a *Flying Camp* [italics added by author for emphasis] be immediately established in the Middle Colonies?

A. Unanimously approved of.

Q. How many should the *Flying Camp* consist of?

A. Ten thousand men.

Q. From whence and in what proportions are the troops to come that are to form the *Flying Camp*?

A. From Pennsylvania 6,000, Maryland 3,400, lower Counties 600; total 10,000.

Q. Is the present establishment sufficient for the Southern Colonies?

A. The present force is sufficient, except in South Carolina and Georgia, where it appears to this Committee that an additional force is necessary.

Q. For how long a time is the Militia to be engaged?

A. To the 1st of December, unless sooner discharged by Congress.

A. From the day of their marching from home; and they are to be allowed one penny a mile, lawful money, in lieu of rations, for traveling expenses, and one day's pay for every twenty miles between home and the general rendezvous, going and returning.

The Committee are of opinion that an animated address be published, to impress the minds of the people with the necessity of their now stepping forward to save their country, their freedom, and property.

That it be earnestly recommended to the Assemblies, Conventions, and Committees of Safety in the United Colonies, to fall upon the most effectual means of removing the stocks, grain, and meal, from such parts of their respective Provinces as are invaded, or are in imminent danger of being invaded the enemy.

It is the opinion of this Committee that two Provincial Brigadiers General be employed in the Canada Department – one from Massachusetts, and one from Connecticut. That four Provincial Brigadiers General be employed in the New York Department – one from

Massachusetts, one from Connecticut, one from New York, and one from New Jersey.

It is also the opinion of this Committee that three Brigadiers General be employed for the Flying Camp—two from Pennsylvania, and one from Maryland; that the said Brigadiers General be appointed by the respective Colonies above mentioned.

Your Committee further recommend that the Departments of Commissary General, Quartermaster General, Adjutant General, & c., be under one head, to whom all Returns and Reports are to be made.

That the Engineers' pay be increased.

That a Resolve of Congress be passed for punishment of Spies found in any of the Continental Camps.

That the Flying Camp be under the command of such Continental General Officers as the Commander-in-Chief shall direct.

That the Commander-in-Chief be authorized to form and fix such Magazines of Provisions and Military Stores as he may judge necessary.

That the General be authorized to direct the building as many Fire Rafts and Galleys as may be necessary and suitable for the immediate defence of the Post at New York and Hudson's River.[18]

Genesis

General Washington had been considering the idea of establishing a unit similar to what we would today call a "rapid response" force. He broached the idea of forming such a unit as early April 20th 1776 to the "Committee of Safety of New York." He wrote,

I have now to request the favor of your information, in what manner and in what time, a Body of 2000 to 2500 Militia, might be collected from this Colony for actual service, upon a sudden Emergency. ... common prudence does nevertheless dictate the expediency of a preconcerted Plan for calling them in, that in case of necessity they may be drawn together in proper corps, without tumult or disorder... with the utmost expedition. This will not be the case, if men are not regularly embodied and notified that they are to step forth at a moment's warning.

The General envisioned a rapid response force, ready to march upon the receipt of signals announcing the approach of the enemy fleet. He presents that "a mode of proceeding of a similar kind, concerted with Jersey would bring in a reinforcement speedily and without those irregularities and unnecessary Expences, which but to frequently attend the movement of Militia."[19] His concept would eventually encompass New York and New Jersey.

In an April 24th letter to the "Legislature or Committee of Safety of New Jersey" he commends the Militia for having "stepped forward in defence of their Country." He suggests that "the Militia of that Province be put under such regulations. As will enable them to give their aid at the very time it may be wanted and without the least delay possible." He notes that under the "present regulation, it will take at least a fortnight to Assemble and embody" the Militia. Concluding with "it seems absolutely necessary that there be a resolution of your Congress or Committee of Safety, for alloting a particular

---

[18] Force, *Archives* 4th Ser, Vol. 6. *Report of the Committee appointed to confer...*, 1686.
[19] George Washington. *The Writings of...* . Vol. 4, 497-498.

number of your Militia to March on the first Notice of the approach of the Enemy; the Detachment from each Regiment should be fixed upon, who should March to certain places of rendesvous, on the first Alarm by regulated signals." [20]

The General followed his earlier letter to New York with one to Governor Jonathan Trumbull on April 26th, commenting "It appears to me expedient, that some mode should be adopted, without loss of time by this, your, and the Jersey, Government, for throwing in immediate succours, upon the apearance of the Enemy or any case of emergency." He informs Governor Trumbull of having written to the New Jersey authorities "upon the subject" and makes the same recommendations to the New York leadership. He reflects that "The benfits flowing from a timely Succor being too obvious for repetition; I shall propose, with all possible deference, for your consideration, whether it will not be advisable to have some select Corps of Men appointed, under proper Officers, in the Western Parts of your Government, to repair to this place, on the earliest notice from the General or Officer Commanding here, of the appearance of an Enemy." [21] Reflected are Washington's earliest conceptions of creating a force of regulated, established troops capable of quickly responding to events. The logistics involved necessitated that such a unit would have to be permanently enrolled and settled into camps in an on-call basis. The whole command needing to be placed under the authority of a single, specifically assigned, commander.

All of which were arrangements that the current militia practices couldn't support. There was uncertainty of how long it would take to assemble a body of militia comprising about 2,000 troops. He cites that it could take "at least a fortnight [two weeks] to Assemble" the Militia. Nor does he seem to be aware of any existing "preconcerted Plan for calling them" together. There were expected "irregularities" to be involved and he cited the expected "unnecessary expenses" associated with calling out the Militia. He was looking for a means of providing a "reinforcement speedily" without the travails to be expected. This then is the genesis of General Washington's Flying Camp concept. He recognized the need and attempted to persuade the States to take efforts to raise such a command. His initial ideas would evolve into a broader concept, combining the "mobile reserve" and necessary "reinforcement speedily," with the need of defending the highly vulnerable New Jersey arena. He envisioned the Flying Camp would eventually serve as a rapid response, mobile reserve acting as the main deterrent against the British invasion of New Jersey and Pennsylvania.

New Jersey was seen as the first line of defense for the middle colonies. General Washington understood that the Jersey coast provided an easy avenue for the British to

---

[20] Ibid. 509-510.
[21] Ibid. 522-523.

move upon Philadelphia.[22] In his July 3rd letter to John Hancock the General states:" I submit to the Congress...that are to provide men for the Flying Camp... It is a matter of great Importance and will be of serious consequence to have the camp established in case the enemy should be able to possess themselves of this River [Hudson] and cut off supplies of Troops that might be necessary, on certain emergencies, to be sent from hence." [23] His concern was the potential for a British invasion of New Jersey to isolate his forces in New York from the Middle colonies.

In his following letter, written July 4th, he says the Camp is to be placed "in the Neighborhood of Amboy" and notes that "the disaffection of the People at that Place and others not far off, is exceedingly great, and unless it is checked and overawed, it may become more general and be very alarming. The arrival of the enemy will encourage it." He further adds, "It is not unlikely that in a little time they may attempt to cross to the jersey side, and induce many to join them, either from motives of Interest or fear, unless there is a force to oppose them." [24] General Washington was concerned with securing his line of communications and logistics with the colonies to the south of New York. The Flying Camp was the defensive force that would accomplish this essential task. Later on July 17th he explains to John Hancock why he ordered Pennsylvania Militia encamped at Trenton, destined for the Flying Camp, to move forward to Amboy. "For having consulted with sundry Gentlemen I was informed, if the Enemy mean to direct their views towards Pennsylvania, or penetrate the Jersey, their Route will be from near Amboy and either by way of Brunswick or Bound Brook."[25] General Washington wanted his forces in strength at the key location he deduced Amboy to be. It is clear that he saw the Flying Camp as a major defensive force consolidated upon the flank of the enemy.

The recommendations for the Flying Camp included 10,000 soldiers primarily being provided by the middle colonies of Pennsylvania, Maryland and Delaware; the length of service to extend to December1st; three Brigadier Generals were to be employed for the unit; and that General Washington appoint the commanding Generals for the Flying Camp. [26] These initial recommendations were debated and approved by Congress only "after some time spent thereon." Even more time was needed "to take into their further consideration the Reports of the Committee of Conference" and the remaining recommendations. Congress received the report on May 29th and the following day resolved to refer the issues to a "Committee of the Whole."

In this action the President of the Congress left his chair and all delegates were then considered as part of a larger committee. The formalities of protocol and procedure in Congress were set aside. Records indicate that once again "sometime was spent thereon "in consideration of the report. While some of the minor points regarding "Fire-Rafts, Row-Galleys, Armed Boats, and Floating Batteries" for protecting New York were quickly approved; [27] major issues regarding the Flying Camp remained unresolved. It was necessary to defer these till another sitting of the Committee of the Whole. Repeatedly from May 31st thru June 3rd the Committee assembled to discuss the report. On June 3rd Congress "*Resolved.* That a Flying-Comp (sic) be immediately established in the Middle Colonies, and that it consist of ten thousand men. To complete which number, *Resolved,*

---

[22]Joseph M. Waterman. *With Sword and Lancet: The Life of General Hugh Mercer.* (Richmond VA: Garrett & Massie.1941).106.
[23] George Washington. *The Writings of...* Vol. 5. 215.
[24] Ibid 220.
[25] Ibid.295
[26] Force, *Archives* 4th Ser, Vol. 6. *Report of the Committee appointed to confer...,*1688.
[27] Ibid, 1691-1692.

That the Colony of *Pennsylvania* be required to furnish, of their militia 6,000, *Maryland,* of their militia 3,400, [and] *Delaware* Government of their Militia, 600. *Resolved.* That the Militias be engaged to the 1st day of December next, unless sooner discharged by Congress." [28] Thus the Flying Camp was born. It would have a short existence filled with trial, tribulation, failure, and glory.

---

[28] Ibid, 1696.

Chapter 2
Spirits from the Vastly Deep

The Flying Camp was intended to provide "a pool of men or units, which would serve as a reserve force for emergencies for the Continental Army."[29] It was a pool that was never completely filled and was often drained of resources. Established by Congressional resolution on June 3rd, the Flying Camp would never take full flight, being more of a "fleeting camp."[30] The Committee of the Whole would meet several times over the next month to resolve tabled points. Among the recommendations approved was the one for employing three Brigadier Generals in the Flying Camp. Also resolved was the issue of granting General Washington the authority to appoint the commanding Generals. Little appears on the subject in the congressional record during the rest of June, 1776. Congress was beleaguered with a sundry list of matters demanding their attention. Much time and debate was given to the declaring of independence from Britain. Matters of great concern regarding the deteriorating conditions in Canada occupied much of their attention. Concerns about the use of the Indians in service of the Colonies were brought forth. A delegation of Chiefs from the Six Nations was received and ceremonies included the giving of gifts and speeches from both sides.

One significant accomplishment was the establishment of a "Committee of Congress ... by the name of a Board of War and Ordnance." The appointed members of the new Board of War were John Adams, Benjamin Harrison, James Wilson, and Edward Rutledge; four of the five original members of the Committee of Conference. [31] In effect, the Committee had evolved into the Board of War.

Among the many issues fielded by the Board of War was the constantly pressing need for troops to fill the Army's ranks. The Congress and its Board of War held only limited powers. "Busy making laws it could not enforce, voting money it could not raise" it was also unable to assemble the armies it needed to raise. [32] In raising troops for the cause Congress found itself calling "spirits from the vastly deep."[33] General Washington's always pressing concern for soldiers to fill the ranks would often find him fishing from that same "vastly deep." The serious concerns over the defense of New York played heavily on the minds of the Commander-in-Chief and his generals.

---

[29] Samuel Newland, *The Pennsylvania Militia: The Early Years 1669-1792,* (Anneville, PA: Pennsylvania National Guard Association, 1997), 141.
[30] William Addleman Ganoe, *The History of the United States Army* (New York: D Appleton, 1924), 27.
[31] Force, *Archives* 4th Ser, Vol. 6. 1703-1704.
[32] Ganoe. 27.
[33] Ibid, 27.

LORD STIRLING.

Correspondence between Washington and his field commanders expressed a sense of urgency about gathering and transferring troops where needed. General William "Lord Stirling" Alexander wrote to the New Jersey Committee of Safety on March 23rd of the "necessity of every Province, contiguous to New-York, exerting themselves in sending troops to this place to assist in fortifying and defending it." [34] He was responding to General William Thompson in New York who had implored him to contact the various State committees. It was hoped the States would order militia for the "necessity of sending a number of troops to this place as soon as possible, as it is very probable that General Howe will endeavor to possess himself of the city." [35] The British strategy for conquering the colonies did focus upon New York and the Hudson River. This strategy and the British experience in America in 1776 must be reviewed to permit a better understanding of the Flying Camp.

"Villainy and maddness…"

The British government's goal was to defeat the insurgency and return the colonies to the subjugation of the Crown. The Declaration of Independence fanned the flames of conflict, raising the temperature of the simmering cauldron of conflict from a bubbling dissention to a boiling revolution. Ambrose Serle, the secretary to Admiral Richard Lord Howe wrote in his journal about the declaration, "It proclaims the villainy and maddness of these deluded people."[36] The brothers, Major General Sir William and Admiral Richard Lord Howe, would play significant roles in dealing with this perceived "maddness."

---

[34] Force, *Archives* 4th Ser, Vol. 6. 475.
[35] Ibid. 475.
[36] Michael Pearson. *Those Damned Rebels: the American Revolution as Seen Through the Eyes of the British.*(New York: G.P. Putnam's Sons, 1972). 155.

The Howe's came to America with dual and somewhat conflicting purposes. As the senior British commanders of the Army and Navy they were charged with the military goal of defeating the insurgents. As diplomats, they were also commissioned to achieve a peaceful resolution of the conflict and reinstate the previous Anglo-American relationship. This dual role, tempered by their personal and political positions, would prove detrimental to the British goal, and come to be of service to the American cause.

The British occupation of Staten Island, and later Long Island, provided a solid base of operations from which General Howe could launch an offensive against the Americans. The British enjoyed supremacy of the sea lanes around New York. With such advantages why didn't General Howe cross into New Jersey ?

General William Howe

By first view it appears the British enjoyed having overwhelming forces available and could have moved and struck without concern. Eventually, General Howe did have the largest British force ever to assemble in the Americas available to him. He has been faulted by some historians for missed opportunities and military blunders in his efforts to quell the rebellion. Some believe that had he launched his campaign thirty to sixty days earlier he may have successfully conquered New York, New Jersey, and Pennsylvania.

Such a devastating blow may have snuffed out the flickering flame of revolt, and the lights of many of our founding fathers. But the consequences of time, travel, distance, and logistics impacted Howe's ability to effectively use his forces in an early onslaught. These aspects, combined with the conflicting roles of military commander and diplomat, temporarily sidelined a rapid military offensive. The delays were not all of his making. The staggered arrival of forces, long lines of supply, and local lack of resources all played a part in his decision process. [37] The march of time shrouds the view of the events and the situation the British faced in New York in 1776.

General Howe's forces arrived in the colonies in piecemeal fashion over the summer of 1776. His regiments came from Halifax Canada, the British Isles, and from South Carolina. He initially landed on Staten Island on July 2nd, with 9300 troops from Canada. On July 12th he was joined by his brother, Admiral Lord Howe, coming from England with 150 ships and more reinforcements. Following later were arrivals of German Mercenaries and more British troops. General Henry Clinton's command returned from the failed Charleston expedition, arriving in New York on August 12th. With that influx General Howe had a combat strength of 24,464 fit soldiers; an additional 10,000 sailors were available under the command of Admiral Lord Howe. On August 27th the General launched his first major offensive against the Americans on Long Island. [38] The General's ability to launch this assault though was not easily gained or fully sustained.

As in every war and all bureaucracies there is opportunity for scoundrels to profit from illicit practices. The British Army in the 1770's was no exception. One scoundrel was a Commissary General Chamiers. The impact of his affairs seriously hampered General Howe's efforts and "frequently resulted in a dearth of provisions that was alarming to the generals in America and that severely affected the conduct of the war."[39] As early as December 1775, while in Boston, General Howe wrote to the Treasury board; "I am in great pain from small quantities of provisions in store.... "Writing to Lord Dartmouth, British statesman and Secretary to the Colonies 1772-1775, Howe states: " The small quantities of Provisions in store ... fill me with alarms...if... ships should not arrive before the latter End of this month... troops [shall be placed] upon short allowance[rations]."[40]

Captain Frederich von Muenchhausen, a Hessian liaison officer assigned to the General, noted that the British saw New Jersey as a place to "afford quarters and supplies for a large force." [41] The pressing need for provisions, aggravated by an extended and ineffective line of supply, forced the Army to survive off the land. This created a burden which the British Army struggled under throughout the war. The logistical problems, coupled with the staggered arrival of his forces, would influence General Howe's conduct of the war through the time of the existence of the Flying Camp.

Every army in the field has had to deal with logistical and strength issues as General Howe faced. While contending with his own such problems he also had to consider the strategic and tactical matters facing him in New York. The British had the

---

[37] Edward E. Curtis. *The Organization of the British Army in the American Revolution.* (New Haven: Yale Univ. Press, 1926), 101.
[38] Boatner. 798
[39] Curtis. 100.
[40] Ibid. 100-101.
[41] Captain Frederich von Muenchhausen. *At General Howe's Side 1776-1778:the diary of Howe's aide de camp.....* . Ernest Kipping and Samuel Smith translators. (Monmouth Beach NJ: Philip Freneau Press, 1974). 57.

significant advantage of naval superiority. It faced only a limited American naval presence. Yet the British Navy could not be everywhere at all times. The influence of winds and tides limited the sailing vessels of the time. These conditions affected their employment in military operations. Even though the British Navy faced a lesser foe it wasn't immune to assault. American artillery positioned along the shores represented a danger to vessels operating on the rivers and close in shore on larger waterways. British ships had to beware of obstructions place in the rivers and watchful for the appearance of fire-boats deployed by the Americans. As we see next, these were not the only hazards facing the Royal Navy.

Always an innovative people, Americans continually endeavor to find new, more efficient means to accomplish their goals. A sidelight in this discussion is the efforts of David Bushnell. He was an inventor of a man-propelled submarine called the "American Turtle." It was a top shaped craft, built of oak beams and said to look like two turtle shells joined together. The craft proved water tight and functional yet never sank a warship. [42] A report of an assault by the British Navy up the North River on October 9th 1776 interestingly mentions the device. During this assault the attacking vessels "were briskly cannonaded from *Fort Washington* and *Fort Constitution* (Lee). The enemy captured a schooner and sunk a sloop which had on board the machine invented by and under the direction of a Mr. *Bushnell,* intended to blow up the *British* ships. This machine was worked under water. It conveyed a magazine of powder, which was to be fixed under the keel of a ship... Mr. *Bushnell* had great confidence of its success, and had made several experiments which seemed to give him countenance; but its fate was truly a contrast to its design."[43]

"American Turtle", Image from the U.S. Navy.

General Howe had other factors to consider besides the role and service of his supporting naval forces. The employment of his land forces against the Americans must have engendered much consideration. He was facing an army which had bested him in the siege of Boston. It had bloodied him severely in the Battles of Breed and Bunker Hills. The same Army had then compelled the temporary withdrawal of his forces from the Colonies. These encounters would obviously not be forgotten. The General had to be a

---

[42] Boatner.147-148.
[43] Peter Force, Ed. *A Documentary History of the United States of America from the Declaration of Independence, July 4, 1776 to the Definitive Treaty of Peace with Great Britain, September 3, 1783,* American Archives: Fifth Series, Volumes 1/2/3, [Hereafter known as Force, *Archives,* 5th Ser, Vols. 1/,2/,3] (Washington: M. St Claire Clarke & Peter Force, 1848), Vol. 2, 961 n.

little wary of his foe.   He wasn't facing a highly trained or organized army but it was a force that had proven ready and capable of giving a good fight.

In selecting Staten Island as his early base of operations in the New York area he occupied a central position. He had ready access to several avenues of assault against the American forces. He was fairly secure in his island base protected by surrounding waters and the British Navy. On the other side of the coin though, he was surrounded by an increasing number of foes, securing and developing defenses against his possible assault against key points. He faced General Washington's main army, initially on Long Island, later on the mainland of New York. A second, growing force composed of the Flying Camp and the Militia, neighbored him in New Jersey. He had to consider that an assault against one would possibly expose him to an attack by the second. Creating a circumstance where he might have to fight on two fronts. Alternatively, he may have chosen to launch his main offensive against General Mercer in New Jersey. Then he would have had to consider that General Washington would move south from New York, against his flank or rear. This could have been a fatal error, repeating the result that occurred earlier in Boston. General Howe chose otherwise, embarking upon the assault against General Washington's main army. What role the defensive measures, forces, and command of General Mercer had on this decision is unknown.

The spirits aroused

The Americans correctly recognized the strategic value of New York City. They surmised it was the focus of British strategy for the 1776 campaigns in America. General Howe brought the army in Halifax Nova Scotia to the city, along with General Clinton's small force in the Carolinas. Additionally a large number of British Regulars and German mercenaries came from Europe. He planned to move up the Hudson River to join smaller forces moving south from Canada. This would hopefully have divided the colonies allowing for the reactionary New England area to be subdued. The southern colonies were then expected to follow in submission.[44]

The Colonists concluded that defending New York City and Fort Ticonderoga would require a two-to-one superiority in troops. Anticipating the British would use 10,000 men against Fort Ticonderoga and 12,500 to seize New York City, Congress determined that the Northern Department would need 20,000 soldiers. General Washington's main army would need 25,000 men. Congress called upon the states to provide 30,000 militia members to help achieve these demands. Six thousand were summoned to defend Fort Ticonderoga, 13,800 for the defense of New York City and 10,000 more for the Flying-Camp. [45]

The threat became reality on June 25th as the British vanguard appeared off the coast of Sandy Hook, New Jersey. By June 28th one hundred-thirty ships lay in the lower bay of New York. On July 2nd British troops landed, unopposed, on Staten Island. Come August General Howe's forces would muster over thirty thousand troops, ten ships of the line and twenty frigates bearing in total 1200 cannons.[46] First word of the British arrival to reach General Washington appears to be in a letter from Lieutenant Joseph Davison of the armed sloop *Schuyler,* dated June 27th, 1776. Lieutenant Davison reported the

[44] Robert Middlekauff. *The Glorious Cause: The American Revolution 1763-1789*. Oxford History of the United States, C Van Woodward, Ed. (New York: Oxford Univ. Press, 1982), 336-39.
[45] Robert K. Wright, Jr. Army Lineage Series, *The Continental Army*. (Washington DC: US Army, 1983), 85-86.
[46] Boatner, 798.

capture of four prizes (ships) previously captured by the British Man-of-War *Greyhound*. Information obtained from prisoners indicated General Howe was aboard the *Greyhound*. Additionally, the British prisoners reported that over one-hundred more vessels were to arrive within days. Davison reported that the *Greyhound* had passed them by three days (June 24th) earlier heading towards Sandy Hook. [47] In a letter of June 29th General Washington advised John Hancock, the President of the Congress, that the accounts of Lieutenant Davison "are partly confirmed, and, I dare say, will turn out to be true in the whole."[48] The die was cast and neither side could afford to step back from the brink.

In a July 3rd letter to Congress, General Washington notes the arrival and movement of the British fleet. "Our reinforcement of Militia is but yet small. However, I trust if the enemy make an attack they will meet with a repulse... as an agreeable spirit and willingness for action seem to animate and pervade the whole of our troops." His optimism not with-standing, he stresses "I submit to Congress whether it may not be expedient for them to repeat and press home their requests to the different Governments that are to provide men for the flying-camp, to furnish their quotas with all possible dispatch." He felt it was a "matter of great importance and ... serious consequence" to have the camp established. [49]

The following day General Washington wrote imploring the body "to interest themselves in having the militia raised and forwarded with all possible expedition as fast as any considerable number of men can be collected that are to compose the Flying-Camp." [50] There had been delays in the effort to raise the assigned quotas for the Flying Camp. On July 3rd, John Hancock called upon the Philadelphia Committee to request, "the troops you are raising to form the flying-camp maybe sent ... with the utmost expedition." To expedite the movement Congress ordered troops be sent as "fast as raised" whether as companies, detachments of battalions or complete battalions. John Hancock had implored the Philadelphians to act on their understanding that the "critical and alarming state of our publick affairs" made it unnecessary to "use arguments to press you to a compliance with any resolves of Congress calculated to promote the cause of liberty in the United Colonies of *America*."[51]

John Hancock's July 4th reply to General Washington informed him of the efforts taken by the Congress to establish the Flying-Camp. "To the unhappy confusions that have prevailed in this Colony [Pennsylvania] must principally be ascribed the delays that have hither to attended that salutary measure" of the establishment of the Flying-Camp.

[47] Force, *Archives* 4th Ser, Vol. 6. 1111
[48] Ibid, 1134.
[49] Ibid, 1234.
[50] Ibid, 1264.
[51] Ibid, 1230.

He endeavored to reassure the General that "things will now take a different turn as the contest to keep possession of power is now at an end, and a new model of government, equal to the exigencies of our affairs, will soon be adopted, agreeably to the recommendation of Congress to the United Colonies." In an apparent effort to encourage General Washington, Hancock requested him "to appoint a proper officer for the command of the Flying-Camp, and persons to supply them with rations." He further commented that he had written to several [state] committees and requested the expedient movement of their troops for the Flying-Camp. [52] The events in Pennsylvania will be examined in depth as we focus on that State's role in the Flying Camp.

John Hancock's letter to the Maryland Convention imparts a different tone than his reassuring message to General Washington. He reflects a state of distress developing over the defense of New York City. He mentions "received intelligence which renders it absolutely necessary that the greatest exertions should be made to save our country from being destroyed by the hand of tyranny. General *Howe* having taken possession of *Staten Island* ... I am directed by Congress to request you will proceed immediately to inbody your militia for establishment of the Flying-Camp, and march them... to *Philadelphia*. ...I do, therefore, most ardently beseech and request you, in the name and by the authority of Congress, as you regard your own freedom, and as you stand engaged by the solemn ties of honor to support the common cause, to strain every nerve to send forward your Militia." He expresses to the Maryland Convention that their action "will prove the salvation of your country" and that the "loss of this campaign will inevitably protract the war." (Author's note: a prophetic statement in the least) He says further "you will not lose a moment in carrying into effect this requisition with zeal, spirit, and dispatch ... required by the critical situation." [53]

General Washington best summarized the response needed in his July 4th letter. "It behooves us to prepare in the best manner; and I submit again to Congress ... the propriety" of taking action and among other efforts "raising the flying-camp with all possible dispatch."[54] Reminding John Hancock that "This I have mentioned in my letters ... but think proper to repeat ... being more and more convinced of the necessity." [55]

Efforts to establish the Flying Camp gained momentum in early July as State governments responded to the Congressional resolves regarding the Militia and Flying Camp. Various Congressional appointments to the organization were being approved. On July 8th a Deputy Quartermaster General, Clement Biddle, was appointed. A Deputy Mustermaster-General, Johnathan B. Smith was selected the following day. Other actions included a resolve to advance one month's pay to those Militia members enrolled in the Flying Camp.[56]

On July 10th, General Washington, responding to John Hancock's "Favors of the 4th and 6th instant," expresses "It is with great pleasure that I hear the Militia from *Maryland,* the *Delaware* Government, and *Pennsylvania,* will be in motion every day to form the Flying-Camp. It is of great importance, and should be accomplished with all

---

[52] Ibid, 1258.

[53] Ibid,1258.

[54] Ibid, 1265-66.

[55] Ibid, 1264.

[56] Peter Force, Ed. *A Documentary History of the United States of America from the Declaration of Independence, July 4, 1776 to the Definitive Treaty of Peace with Great Britain, September 3, 1783,* American Archives: Fifth Series, Volume I/2/3, [Hereafter known as Force, *Archives,* 5th Ser, Vol. 1/2/3] (Washington: M. St Claire Clarke & Peter Force, 1848), Vol. 1, 1569-1570.

possible dispatch." He especially notes the role and response of the Pennsylvania government as such difficulty had occurred in its effort to raise the troops. "The readiness and alacrity with which the Committee of Safety of *Pennsylvania* and the other conferees have acted, in order to forward the associated Militia of that state to the *Jerseys* for service, till the men to compose the Flying-camp arrive, strongly evidence their regard to the common cause, and that nothing on their part will be wanting to support it."

The General mentions that actions would be taken to provide for the reception of the Militia. He reports that a "proper officer will be appointed to command it" [the Flying Camp]. [57] He further comments that "General [Hugh] *Mercer* is now in the *Jerseys*, for the purpose of receiving and ordering the Militia coming from the Flying-Camp." [58] This confirms an earlier indication that the energetic Mercer would be the commander of the Flying Camp. In a July 4th letter to Brigadier General William Livingston of New Jersey, General Washington had advised "I must refer you to General Mercer whose judgement and experience may be depended upon."[59]

Congress appointed Hugh Mercer as a Brigadier General on June 5th, 1776. He was immediately ordered to report to General Washington's New York Headquarters. A longtime friend, the General had recommended him to the Congress for the appointment and assignment to New York. [60] He had been born near Aberdeen, Scotland around 1723. He served as an assistant surgeon in the Highland Army under "Bonnie" Prince Charley," Charles Edward, Prince of Scotland. After the defeat of the Scots, Mercer had to leave Scotland in 1746. He immigrated to America, settling into a practice as a doctor near the present town of Mercersburg, in now Franklin County, Pennsylvania. He served in the provincial militia in 1755 during the French and Indian War. He rose to the rank of Lieutenant Colonel and participated in the Battle of Kittanning in 1756 where he was wounded.[61] General Mercer's energy, experience, and devotion to the cause surely contributed to his selection.

---

[57] Ibid, 173.

[58] Ibid, 174.

[59] Waterman. 110.

[60] Freeman. *George Washington*, 107n.

[61] William B. Reed. "Oration Delivered on the Ocassion of the Reinterment of the Remains of General Hugh Mercer Before the St. Andrews and Thistle Society Thursday November 26th, 1840." (Philadelphia: Press of A. Waldie, 1840). *Pamphlets in American History*. "Miscellany of Revolutionary War Biographies." Group 1, (microform).(Sanford, NC:Microfilming Corporation of America,1979). No. RW ???

John Hancock confirmed Congress' approval of the appointment to command the Flying Camp in a letter of July 14th ; "Sir: The Congress having been informed by General *Washington*, that he had given the command of the Flying Camp and Militia in *New Jersey*, to you, and for that purpose you were stationed in the *Jerseys,* I have it in charge from Congress to empower and direct you to march such of the Militia and Flying-Camp to *Brunswick* or other places as may be conducive to the publick service..." [62] Congress was thus on record as granting General Mercer the authority to deal with the various state militias as necessary regarding his command. Writing to his commander that same day, General Mercer exhibits his drive and daring in proposing offensive actions against the British. Using recently arrived Pennsylvania Riflemen he felt "a favorable opportunity may probably offer to surprise the enemy's small posts. Boats may, I think, be procured; and the riflemen would be happy to be so employed. Such an enterprise is not suspected by the enemy, nor believed to be under consideration here. " [63]

General Mercer's enthusiasm for taking the offensive is admirable but his peers and associates was far less optimistic. General Washington forwarded to Congress (July 11th) intelligence obtained from a prisoner relating that Admiral Howe and his fleet were expected hourly. An advance vessel from the fleet had arrived and the "prevailing Opinion [among British troops, author's note] is, that an Attack will be made immediately on their Arrival." [64] Admiral Lord Howe, the elder brother of General Howe arrived on July12th leading 150 ships transporting thousands of reinforcements for the British. Nearly three-hundred British ships would come to lie in the bays around New York. General Washington, writing to Congress that evening noted, "Several Ships have come in to day, among them one ... we conclude to be Admiral Howe. It is probable they will all arrive in a Day or two and immediately begin their operations."[65]

The arrival of Admiral Howe's fleet heightened the already considerable apprehension existing among the Americans. In Philadelphia, the Continental Congress in the afternoon hours of July 13th, "Adjourned to nine o'clock, on *Monday* next." General Washington's letters of the 11th and 12th apparently arrived that evening. In violation of past practice, the Congress reconvened on the Sabbath, Sunday July 14th. The General's letters "were laid before Congress, and read." The news of Admiral Howe's arrival prompted an immediate response among the delegates.

Among the actions taken was a resolve to forward "20,000 Dollars" to Colonel Clement Biddle, Deputy Quartermaster-General for the use of the Flying Camp and Militia in New Jersey. Colonel Biddle was further ordered to use all means to dispatch supplies including flour, tents, camp kettles, and canteens to the Flying Camp. He was further instructed to employ "Armourers for the Army in *New-Jersey.*" Congress also resolved to direct the "Convention of *New-Jersey* to supply all the Lead they possibly can for the Flying-Camp and Militia." Pennsylvania was requested to supply as "many Musket Cartridges, well balled, as they can possible spare." Orders were dispatched by an "Express" to Colonel F. Lewis in Virginia to forward "all the Lead he can collect at *Fredericksburgh.*" The State of Virginia was to be asked to send as much lead as they could from supplies in Williamsburg. Fifteen to twenty tons of lead from their mines was

---

[62] Force, *Archives*, 5th Ser, Vol. 1. 327.

[63] Ibid, 328.

[64] George Washington. "Letter: George Washington to Continental Congress, July 11,1776." *The Writings of George Washington from the Original Manuscript Sources 1745-1799. The George Washington Papers at the Library of Congress, 1741-1799.* John C. Fitzpatrick, Ed. www.memory.loc.gov (hereafter noted as Washington -LOC-Online).

[65] Ibid, Letter: July 12, 1776.

to be sent to Philadelphia as soon as possible. Orders were to be sent to General Mercer directing the movement of the Militia and Flying Camp, as available, to Brunswick or other places as judged necessary. The Pennsylvania government was directed to have all British officers held prisoner in Philadelphia transferred to other locations outside the city. The commanding officer in Pennsylvania was directed to "issue fresh orders, and exert himself, to forward the immediate march of the Militia to *New-Jersey.*"[66] The rapid and broad-based actions of the Continental Congress on that July Sunday reflects their expectations that major engagements were to occur forthwith.

The pending invasion of New York and the slow response to the filling of the quotas for the Flying Camp compelled Congress to act. On July 15th it appointed a committee to "consider the propriety and means of augmenting the Flying-Camp." The committee members included Thomas Jefferson of Virginia, Thomas Stone of Maryland, George Read from Delaware, John Morton of Pennsylvania, and Richard Stockton from New Jersey.[67] Abraham Clark of New Jersey would be added on July 29th. John Hancock wrote to General Washington "you will perceive your letters of the 11th and 12th instant have been received, and laid before Congress, and that in consequence thereof, they have taken such measures as are calculated to expedite the raising the Flying-Camp, and to furnish them with articles of the greatest use and necessity." He explained that he had written to General Mercer and others giving orders "to the proper persons to have executed."[68]

Among Hancock's letters of July 15th is a particularly interesting communication to the Convention of New Jersey. It affords presenting if only to show the degree of effort and extremes to which the Americans were prepared to go to in support of the cause. "Gentlemen: The article of lead being so essentially necessary for our Army, and the propriety of every Colony being furnished with it so evident, that the Council of Safety of this Colony [Pennsylvania] recommended to the inhabitants to spare the lead weights from their windows, by which means they have been furnished with a considerable quantity, which has been run into ball; and part of which the Council of Safety here having willingly spared, and is now on the way to the Jerseys"[69]

The following day, July 16th, the Congress took a step which would have a direct impact on several units and particularly the Flying Camp. Among its deliberations it "*Resolved,* That General Washington be desired to call to his assistance, at New York, two thousand of the men who have marched into New Jersey to form the flying camp; and that the convention of New Jersey be requested immediately to supply their places with an equal number of the militia of that state."[70] The impact of this suggestion to the Commander – in – Chief would affect thousands of troops and several states.

In a July 17th letter to General Washington, John Hancock informs him that "upwards of a thousand troops from *Maryland* are now in this city, on their way to join the Flying-Camp in *New-Jersey.* They are an exceedingly fine body of men, and will begin their march this day."[71] However on the same day he writes to the commander of the

---

[66] Force, *Archives*, 5th Ser, Vol. 1. 1556-1557.

[67] Ibid, 1578.

[68] Ibid, 346.

[69] Ibid, 346.

[70] Continental Congress of the United States, 2nd Session. *A Century of Lawmaking for a New Nation.* United States Congressional Documents, Journals of the Continental congress, Volume 5. (July 16th , 1776). HTTP://[Online]:http://memory.loc.gov/ll/lljc/005/0100/0100565.gif 16 September 2004.

[71] Force, *Archives*, 5th Ser, Vol. 1. 387.

Maryland contingent, Colonel William Smallwood. "Sir: I have in charge from Congress to direct that you, as soon as possible, march the troops from *Maryland*, now in this city [Philadelphia], to *New-York*, and there put yourself under the command of General *Washington*. The exigency of the service requiring as speedy a junction as possible of your troops with those at *New-York*, I recommend you use all dispatch in your power."[72] It seems the President of Congress was intentionally bending the details slightly in reporting the movement of the Maryland troops as being on that day. While at the same time he is directing the commander of the contingent to move as soon as possible.

Difficulties in forging the Flying Camp still beleaguered the Congress and General Washington. On Friday, July 19th Congress acted to accelerate the efforts to provide the troops promised from Pennsylvania. It "*Resolved*, That it be earnestly recommended to the Convention of *Pennsylvania* to hasten, with all possible expedition, the march of the Associators into *New-Jersey*, agreeable to a former request of Congress." The movement of the Maryland troops then in Philadelphia was also pursued by a resolution "That the delegates of *Maryland* be directed to inform the Commanding Officer of the *Maryland* troops that Congress expect he will immediately march with his Troops to *New-York*." Other matters taken up by the Congress that day included the assignment of Samuel Griffin as Deputy Adjutant General for the Flying Camp.[73]

The committee appointed to review and develop measures for increasing the Flying Camp brought in its report on July 20th. Taking the report into consideration, Congress resolved to enact three of the recommendations:

1. The "Convention of *Pennsylvania* was requested to augment their quota for the Flying-Camp, with four Battalions of Militia."
2. It was resolved that "Brigadier-General *Lewis* be directed to order two Battalions of the Continental Troops, in *Virginia,* to march, with all possible despatch, to the Flying –Camp, in *New Jersey*. "
3. Finally, the Convention of New Jersey was requested "to raise, for the said Flying-Camp, three Battalions of Militia."[74]

The New Jersey leadership initially exhibited some reluctance, saying they had recently sent 2,000 militiamen to the Flying-Camp. [75] The state convention though would soon accede to the request. From Virginia, General Lewis reported that the First and Third Continental Battalions were marching. [76] Pennsylvania would resolve to "fix the proportion of the city [Philadelphia] and the several counties... towards composing the four additional Battalions required by congress for the Flying-Camp."[77] The arrival of British forces at New York had rattled the Congress and its military command. Desperate measures were required to meet the inevitable assault. Efforts to raise the Flying Camp encompassed five states; from Delaware to Virginia. The number of troops needed rose from 10,000 to over 12,000.

A number of people, at both the Continental and the State levels, were involved in creating the Flying Camp. To this point we've had an overview of the circumstances

---

[72] Ibid, 388.
[73] Ibid, 1584.
[74] Ibid, 1586.
[75] Force, *Archives* 4th Ser, Vol. 6. 1653.
[76] Force, *Archives,* 5th Ser, Vol. 1. 1053.
[76] Force, *Archives,* 5th Ser, Vol. 2. 8.
[77] Force, *Archives,* 5th Ser, Vol. 2. 8.

and events prompting the development of the unit. The actions of the Continental leadership to authorize its creation and organization have also been examined. Although only three States were initially involved: Pennsylvania, Maryland, and Delaware; eventually six States would provide men and means for the Flying Camp. For a more complete picture it is necessary to look at the efforts and contributions of each of these States.

Chapter 3
Delaware

"Here's the Loyal son... "[78]

Prior to the Revolution the colony of Delaware, originally known as the Lower Counties of Pennsylvania, supported a population of nearly 37,000 citizens. The small population limited the number of troops it could furnish.[79] Delaware was tasked by the Continental Congress in a Committee of Conference Report of May 29th that from "the lower counties 600" was required for the Flying Camp. [80] The enlistment of Delaware troops was approved on June 3rd. The response was enthusiastic and In 1776 the State would provide a total of 754 troops for the cause. By the end of the war's second year it had supplied four units: two regiments, one battalion, and a partisan company.[81]

Earlier in December 1775, the Congress resolved that one battalion was to be raised in the low counties of Delaware.[82] Quickly responding to the call, a regiment of Delaware troops was established in January 1776. On January 19th the "council of safety of the three lower counties on Delaware, having recommended sundry gentlemen for field officers, of the battalion ordered to be raised in said colony, the Congress proceeded to the choice , when the following gentlemen were chosen as the senior regimental commanders : John Haslet, Esqr, Colonel and Gunning Bedford, Esqr, lieutenant Colonel."[83] In addition to these officers a John McPhearson was elected as a Major in the unit. He would however be killed in action at the Battle for Quebec on December 31st, 1775, where he was serving as an aid to General Montgomery. Word of his loss had not been received at the time of his election to the position in the Delaware Regiment. A subsequent election of Thomas McDonough was made on March 22, 1776. Additional staff selected included James Tilton as Surgeon and Joseph Montgomery as Chaplain. [84] The Delaware regiment would also be referred to as Colonel Haslet's Regiment. John William Haslet (spellings include Haslett, Hazlet) was born in Ireland, where he studied for the Presbyterian ministry but later became a physician. Immigrating to the America's, he established a successful medical practice in Delaware. His pre-revolutionary experience included service as a Colonel in the colonial militia and as a member of the Delaware Assembly.[85]

The recruiting of the regiment occurred through January to April of 1776. On March 22nd the Delaware House of Representatives provided "Instructions for Inlisting Men in service of the Delaware Government." These provide an interesting view into the character desired in the soldiers, and that of those wanting such.

---

[78] . George B Hynson and William S. Brown. *Official State Song s: Delaware State Song.* (1925) www. netstate.com/state/symb/song/de-song. 8 August 2005.

[79] Henry Hobart Ballas. *A History of the Delaware State Society of the Cincinnati.* (Wilmington DE: Historical Society of Delaware, 1895), 41.

[80] Peter Force, ed., ", *A Documentary History of the English Colonies in North America from the King's Message to Parliament of March 7,1774 to the Declaration of Independence of the United States.* American Archives: Fourth Series, volume VI. (Hereafter known as Force, *Archives* 4th Ser, Vol. 6)(Washington: M. St. Claire Clarke and Peter Force, 1846), Report of the Continental Congress, May 24, 1776. 1683.

[81] Ballas, 41, 41*n*.

[82] Christopher L Ward. *The Delaware Continentals 1776-1786.* (Willington DE: Historical Society of Delaware, 1941), 4.

[83] Public Archives Commission. *Delaware Archives.* "Military."[henceforth Delaware Archives] (Wilmington DE: Mercantile, 1911, 1974r), Vol. 1, 31.

[84] William G. Whiteley. *The Revolutionary Soldiers of Delaware.* (Wilmington DE: James & Webb, 1875. 10-11.
        A roster of Company grade officers is also included in this work.

[85] Mark Boatner. *Encyclopedia of the American Revolution,* (Mechanicsburg PA: Stackpole Books, 1994), 494.

1. You are to Inlist no Man who is not Able-bodied, healthy and a good Marcher, nor such whose Attachment to the cause of America you have cause to suspect. Young, hearty, robust Men who are tied by Birth, or Family Connections, or Property, to the Country are by much to be preferred.
2. You will have great regard to Moral Character; Sobriety in particular.
3. You are not to inlist any servant or Apprentice.
4. Those who engage in the service shall be inlisted according to the form prescribed by this Assembly.
5. The Commanding Officer of the company shall appoint such Men, Sergeants and Corporals, as recommend themselves by their Ability, Activity and Diligence, and he is to appoint the Drummers and Fifer.
6. You are to be allowed seven shillings and six Pence per Week for the Subsist of Recruits till they arrive at their Station.
7. You are to take Notice that the Muster-Master appointed, is to inspect your Men and reject such as do not answer to your Instructions.
8. You shall be allowed seven shillings and six Pence for each Man you inlist who shall be past on Inspection as Effective, besides the Subsist-Money before, and your Pay.

By Order,

Jas. Booth, clk of Assembly.[86]

An example of the "Form of the Inlistment" cited in item 4 is provided for interest.

I Sheppard Foster do voluntarily inlist myself a Soldier, to serve as such until the first Day of December next, unless sooner discharged by Order of the House of Assembly, or Council of Safety of the Government on Delaware for the Time being, hereby subjecting Myself to such rules and Regulations as are, or shall be made by the House of Assembly, or Council of Safety of said government, for Regulating and governing the forces in the Government. Witness my Hand this 4th Day of April Anno Domini.

Sheppard Foster.

Lt. Wiltbank.
1776 [87]

[86] Delaware Archives. 33.
[87] .Ibid. 34

Colonel Haslet's Regiment (often referred to as a battalion)[88] was created before the establishment of the Flying Camp. Until the intended Delaware Flying Camp emerged the regiment was repeatedly called upon to fill the gap. It provided yeoman service to the revolutionary cause.

The Delaware Regiment, also known as the Delaware Blues, was called "the best uniformed and equipped in the Army of 1776." [89] It was composed of eight companies and numbered eight hundred men. The officers were appointed by the Congress, based on the recommendations of the Delaware Council of Safety. [90] The regiment was eventually assigned to General William (Lord Stirling) Alexander's brigade. Of which it was said, "Washington regarded with peculiar satisfaction." [91] Colonel Haslet's opinion of his unit is best expressed in a letter to Thomas Rodney:

> On *Sunday*, the 25th of *August* last, my regiment was ordered to *Long Island*, in Lord *Stirling's* brigade...On *Tuesday,* the 27th, his brigade, consisting of five regiments... not exceeding five thousand men, were ordered to advance beyond the lines and repulse the enemy. To oppose this small band were seventeen thousand regulars, much better furnished with field-pieces and every other military appointment than we. Several of the regiments were broken and dispersed soon after the first onset. The *Delawares* and *Marylanders* stood firm to the last; and, after a variety of skirmishing, the *Delawares* drew up on the side of a hill, and stood upwards of four hours with ... determined countenance, in close array, their colors flying, ... enemy's artillery playing on them all the while, not daring to advance and attack them, though six times their number and nearly surrounding them. Nor did they think of quitting their station till an express order from the General commanded their retreat... The *Delawares* alone had the honour of bringing off twenty-three prisoners. ...The *Delaware* battalion, officers and men, are respected through out this army.[92]

This earned respect, garnered prior to the above event, had prompted Congress to call upon the Regiment for service in lieu of the yet formed Delaware Flying Camp.

---

[88] The terms battalion and regiment were synonymous at this time and were often interchanged when speaking of the same unit.

[89] Charles M. Lefferts. *Uniforms of the American, British, French and German Armies in the War of American Revolution 1775-1780.*(Old Greenwich CT: WE, Inc. 1971). 26 .

[90] Whiteley. 10-11.

[91] Ward, 17.

[92] Peter Force, Ed. *A Documentary History of the United States of America from the Declaration of Independence, July 4, 1776 to the Definitive Treaty of Peace with Great Britain, September 3, 1783,* American Archives: Fifth Series, Volumes 1/2/3, [Hereafter known as Force, *Archives,* 5th Ser, Vols. 1/,2/,3] (Washington: M. St Claire Clarke & Peter Force, 1848), 5th Ser, Vol. 2. 881-882.

Battle of Long Island. Engraving, 1874, from painting by Alonzo Chappel. 111-SC-96741 [93]

On July 4th John Hancock wrote to the Delaware Assembly imploring them to "imbody your Militia for the establishment of the Flying Camp" and to march immediately for Philadelphia. [94] On July 5th Congress directed that "Colonel Hazlet, of the Battalion in Delaware Government, be ordered to station one Company at *Lewistown*, and to march the remaining seven to *Wilmington*, and there remain until further order of this Congress."[95] Caesar Rodney, Delaware delegate to the Continental Congress, provides an explanation for this movement in a letter dated July 10th to his brother Thomas. He wrote, "Colonel Haslett's battalion (except one company, which is to stay at Lewis) is ordered up to Wilmington, as a security to Philadelphia in absence of their Militia." [96] On July 21st John Hancock provided Colonel Haslet with the further orders of Congress, "Sir: In consequence of a resolution of Congress passed yesterday evening, I am to direct you, immediately and without loss of time after receipt of this, to march with the troops under your command to Philadelphia, there to do duty until the further orders of Congress." [97] The company stationed at Lewistown was to remain there for the time being.

Colonel Haslet's battalion, minus the Lewistown detachment, arrived in the city on August 3rd, 1776. On that same date the Congress ordered the Company "posted at Lewis-town as soon as possible to march to Philadelphia and join their battalion now

---

[93] Pictures of the Revolutionary War. Select Audiovisual Records. National Archives and Records Administration, Washington, DC 20408. http://www.archives.gov/research/american-revolution/pictures/images/revolutionary-war-029.jpg, August 25, 2005.
[16] Force, *Archives*, 5th Ser, Vol. 1. 1258.
[95] Ibid, 1566.
[96] Ibid, 170.
[97] Ibid, 482.

stationed at the barracks in this city."[98] The Delaware Regiment was in Philadelphia but a short time when Colonel Haslett received orders on August 6th that "without loss of time, march your battalion to Amboy, New Jersey. "[99] Staying at Amboy only a few days, the Regiment was ordered to march as part of two thousand troops of the Flying Camp being sent to New York. Colonel Haslet's force would become comrades in arms with Colonel William Smallwood's Maryland regiment. Together, the two units served gallantly in the later New York campaigns.

John Haslet was devoted to the revolutionary cause and bemoaned the results of the battles around New York. In a letter written September 4th while encamped at Kings Bridge he expresses his concerns and thoughts surrounding the earlier events.

> Here are we on the Heights above King's Bridge, exposed to wind, Weather & the Enemy, who appear to have it nearly as much in their Power to cut off our communications as ever. Our army has been once already deranged—Immensity of Labor & Expense thrown away in fortifying L. Island at once abandoned, & N. York soon to be in the same situation, from the superior Number of the British Troops, & the Advantages of their Fleet the City is Indefensible, (you know, Sir, I speak only my own Opinions to those in whom I confide) their throwing men across any part of the N. York Island , easily in their power some where to effect in one night, & digging up a slight intrenchment, effectually reduces the City & all within their Line, to the Dire Necessity of fighting at vast Disadvantage, or Surrendering at Discretion, Dreadfull Alternative! Had Long Island been rendered useless to the Enemy, N. York laid in Ashes, when we were ordered when we were ordered to L. Island, and the Heights between this & Connecticut properly Occupied, the Enemy must have attacked at Disadvantage; or we at Liberty to fight when we pleased, & if worsted, wou'd have had it in our power to retire to the next Adjacent Hill, & obstinately disputed every inch in their Progression this true , this kind of Devastation may be condemned as cruel, but Provinces e'er now have been sacrificed with Applause to the safety of a Kingdom, & what ought not to be done for the Safety of a Continent, the Gen.l I revere, his character for Disinterestedness Patience * fortitude will be had in Everlasting Remembrance; but the vast Burthen appears much too much, his own. Beardless, Youth, & Inexperience Regimentaled are to much about him, the original scheme for the Disposition of the army appears to have been on two Narrow a Scale, & every thing almost sacrificed, or Indangered for the Preservation of N.York & its Invirons, all which deserve from every Honest American Political D—nation. …We expect every moment Something Important here, & hope in our next to fight on more Equal terms, & give you a more pleasing Accompt--…

John Haslet [100]

Colonel Haslet's Regiment had served as the vanguard of Delaware's commitment to the Flying Camp. It would fall to Colonel Samuel Patterson to organize the Delaware Flying Camp. Samuel Patterson was a miller by profession, residing near

---

[98] Ibid, 740.
[99] Ibid, 785.
[100] Delaware Archives, 1391.

Christiana Bridge, Delaware. He appears to have also been a Brigadier General in the Delaware State Militia during his lifetime.[101] What experience he had in military matters before the war isn't known. His experience in raising and commanding the Delaware Flying Camp is not to be envied. The State's effort to raise the quota was initiated in late July, 1776. [102] The unit was expected to serve only until December 1st. Henry Ballas indicates it consisted of eight companies of infantry. [103] It supposedly consisted of nine companies, mustering a reported strength of 480 troops, according to Christopher Ward. [104] There were substantial difficulties involved in raising the full quota. Reluctance and refusal to enlist existed among those subject to service. The inadequacies of the established terms of enlistment, the method of selecting the officers, and perceived poor compensation for service combined to be "fatal to everything like discipline" among the troops.[105] One result of this lack of discipline was the incidents of desertion from the unit. An examination of rosters and rolls from the Battalion indicates that between July and October apparently forty-one individuals deserted. A number though were "taking up & brough back..." to the unit. [106] In August 1776, the Delaware Convention issued a public notice that it had "furnished their quota to the Flying Camp."[107]

Such announcements obviously provided for good public appearances but the realities involved in creating and maintaining a viable military unit were daunting. Colonel Patterson raised and moved his regiment first to Philadelphia, then on to Amboy. While in Philadelphia a near mutiny occurred among the soldiers. Nearly half the regiment laid down their arms in protest over not receiving the same bounty their Pennsylvania comrades were granted. It took the threat of the bayonet and of disarming and arresting them to encourage the rebellious men to march. In his letter to George Reed dated September 19th he wrote "I at last got them down to the wharf, fixed bayonets at the head of it, and sent them off." Colonel Patterson's problems continued as he spent the night in the city with one remaining company. In the morning he awoke to find that all but eleven men of the company had deserted as darkness lay upon the city. To Reed he wrote that "This day I leave this city, thank God! Never man has been so uneasy. [108]

On September 27th, writing from the Flying Camp Headquarters at Amboy, the Colonel reported he had arrived with six companies of the battalion.[109] A letter dated October 6th reflects one more company's arrival. At the time he mentions having 70 men sick, three dead, and one officer ill. Colonel Patterson also questioned a report he had received that Delaware was considering the raising of another battalion. He noted that his unit was under manned; having only 450 troops while a rank and file of the 600 were required. [110]

The Colonel's initial impressions of his battalion raised doubts in his mind about the usefulness of the unit. He comments in one letter that "Had I known the men in general, I would not have went with them. Some few excessive good, others, perhaps, another day may be brave, not at present. In my opinion, that had better have staid at home." He and his men seem to have acclimated to their situation. In a later letter Colonel Patterson writes that "Since they left Philadelphia, the Battalion is sorry for their

---

[101] Whiteley, 17.
[102] Ward, 488.
[103] Ballas, 42.
[104] Ward 488.
[105] Whiteley, 17-18.
[106] Delaware Archives, 67-73.
[107] Force, *Archives*, 5th Ser, Vol. 2. 285.
[108] Whitley, 18.

misbehavior. It was owing to a rascal telling them they were fools to go without their bounty." The time spent in camp, drilling, and training established a rapport and comradely which swayed Colonel Patterson's opinion. By November 4th letter he writes "I have some noble officers in my Battalion, whom I could recommend, if a door open."[111] The Delaware Flying Camp remained at Amboy till mustering out in December 1776. The battalion saw action only once, as part of an expedition led by General Mercer against the British on Staten Island in October.

Colonel Patterson's battalion joined a force of 600, embarking in boats around 8 o'clock that evening. Come daybreak the unit was ashore upon the east end of the island. Colonel Patterson wrote with pride that the force marched with "our battalion in front." The initial objective was bypassed due to the arrival there of unexpected British reinforcements. The assault was redirected at a smaller garrison at Richmond. General Mercer planned to attack at dawn. He divided his force, sending Colonel Patterson along with other units to accomplish a blocking action against a British retreat. The remaining portions of his command were to strike the enemy position at three points. The senior officer commanding Patterson's detachment, a Colonel Griffin, was apparently too eager and ordered the attack to early. Colonel Patterson wrote "We began at it as hard as we could blaze... It not being light [we] had liked to have shot our own people." The engagement lasted near an hour. The casualties were five of the enemy dead, two Americans killed, and four wounded.[112]

In an inspection report dated November 14th, sent from the Headquarters at Perth Amboy, the state of the Battalion is reported to the Delaware Convention.

And as you are enjoined to inquire into the Condition of said Battalion, he [Patterson] informs you, that his Battalion is very badly Cloath'd, and a number of his Blankets were lost on the Expedition on Staten Island and that he has not been able to procure any since so that many of his Battalion is badly off, on that account, but that he has number of spare arms & accoutrements, ... which .... , he will immediately transmit to the Delaware State.

Little resolution of the difficulties facing the commander and men of the Delaware Flying Camp occurred. On December 1st, at the end of their term of service, Colonel Patterson's battalion returned home. A bill of expenses amounting to 2851 pounds, 3 shillings, and 19 pence was later presented to the Delaware Assembly.[113] It is commented that "being undisciplined militia their record was not satisfactory, and they returned to their homes at the expiration of their brief term of service, having had but one slight skirmish with the enemy."[114] This is truly an undeserved and shallow epitaph for the "Loyal son" among them.

---

[109] Force, *Archives*, 5th Ser, Vol. 2, 570.
[110] Ibid. 918.
[111] Whiteley, 18-19.
[112] Ward. 488-489.
[113] Ibid.
[114] Ballas, 42.

Chapter 4
Maryland

"The despot's heel is upon thy shore…"[115]

The Continental Congress had tasked Maryland with providing 3,400 men for the Flying Camp. The Maryland Convention held session on June 25th and considered the request. It was *"Resolved, Unanimously, That this Province will furnish three thousand four hundred and five of its Militia, to form a Flying Camp…according to the request of the Congress in their Resolutions of the 3d day of this instant, June."* Four battalions were to be raised, each composed of nine companies, and each company consisting of ninety men each. The members were to serve until the 1st day of December or till released sooner. [116] The companies of the Maryland contingent were to be raised from fourteen counties (see Table 1). On June 27th Thomas Johnson, Jr. was elected Brigadier-General to command the Maryland Militia and by association those State militia then in the Flying Camp.[117], [118] From August 16th to December 1st Rezin Beall, promoted to Brigadier General, was appointed to serve as the commander of the Maryland Flying Camp.[119] General Thompson would continue to serve as the senior Brigadier General over the Maryland militia until elected as the first Governor of the State. [120]

Counties	Number of companies
St. Mary's, Calvert, Dorchester, Talbot	1 (each)
Charles, Harford, Cecil, Kent, Queen Anne, Caroline	2 (each)
Prince George's	3
Baltimore	4
Anne Arundel	5
Frederick	9

Table 1. County allocations for troops serving in the Maryland Flying Camp.[a]

Difficulties and changes in priority bedeviled the formation of the Flying Camp. The Maryland contingent was not immune to such events. On July 4th, Matthew Tilghman, President of the Maryland Convention, sent to John Hancock the Convention's resolutions for "raising the number of Militia required of this Province for the Flying Camp."[121] Yet, before Tilghman's letter was read before the Congress on July 8th

---

[115] James Ryder Randall. *Maryland , My Maryland.* (April 1861). www. netstate.com/state/symb/song/md-my-md. 8 August 2005.

[116] *American Archives*: Fourth Series, Volume VI. "A Documentary History of the English Colonies in North America from the King's Message to Parliament of March 7,1774 to the Declaration of Independence of the United States." Washington: M. St. Claire Clarke and Peter Force, 1846. 1487-88.

[117] Ibid.1490.

[118] The muster rolls of the companies raised for the Maryland Flying-Camp can be found in *Archives of Maryland: Muster Roll and Other Records of Service of Maryland Troops in the American Revolution*, volume 18. (Baltimore: Maryland Historical Society, 1900). Also available on-line at " www.mdarchives.state.md.us/ ."

[119] George Washington,. "The Diaries of George Washington. Donald Jackson, ed.; Dorothy Twohig, assoc. ed. The Papers of George Washington. Charlottesville: University Press of Virginia, 1978.." *The George Washington Papers at the Library of Congress, 1741-1799.* John C. Fitzpatrick, Ed. Vol. 3 , 232, paragraph 11 n [Online]:www.memory.loc.gov.

[120] Maryland State Archives. *Archives of Maryland (Biographical Series)* "Thomas Johnson 1732-1819 ".(Maryland State Archives Annapois MD). http://www.mdarchives.state.md.us/megafile/msa/speccol/sc3500/sc3520/000700/000743/html/743bio.html. 8 June 2006.

a. Force, *Archives*, 4th Ser, Vol. 6, 1490.

Maryland was called upon to again come to the service of the nation. In another letter to the Maryland Convention Hancock wrote, "I am directed by the Congress to request you will proceed immediately to imbody your Militia for the establishment of the Flying Camp, and march them with all possible expedition, either by battalion, detachments of battalions, or by companies, to the City of *Philadelphia.*"[122] This was necessary because on July 4th Congress had dispatched "militia from *Pennsylvania* to Trenton in haste and to serve until the Flying Camp of ten thousand men could relieve them." [123] In Convention at Annapolis on July 6th, the new request was taken into consideration. Thereupon it was "*Ordered,* That Colonel Smallwood immediately proceed with his Battalion to the City of *Philadelphia....*" Additionally, four independent companies, one each from Talbot, Kent, Queen Anne's, and St. Mary's counties, were also ordered to immediately march to Philadelphia. There the companies were placed under the command of Colonel Smallwood.[124] The Maryland Convention further resolved that the number of Militia and Regulars ordered to Philadelphia be deducted from the quota composing the Flying Camp. [125]

This troop movement prompted further realignments among the Maryland Militia. Units from Annapolis were reassigned to Baltimore to replace the State Regulars sent to Philadelphia. Other difficulties in preparing and dispatching troops to Philadelphia and the Flying Camp were encountered. Equipping the hastily organized units was a difficult task. The required supplies included rifles, cartouche-boxes, bayonets, and tents. [126] The problems involved in obtaining supplies would never be completely overcome. By August 18th, the Maryland Convention was able to advise Congress that their full quota for the Flying Camp was near ready. Though still they had to report that the troops were "lacking only arms" to go to New Jersey.[127]

Maryland State Regulars

On January 1st, 1776 the Maryland Convention resolved that "a sufficient armed force be immediately raised and embodied under proper officers, for the defence and protection of this province." The force was to consist of 1444 men aligned into a battalion of nine companies and an additional seven independent companies. Also, two artillery companies and one company of marines were authorized. A key aspect of the resolutions enacted by the Convention was the empowerment of the Maryland Council of Safety to order these troops to leave the state in support of military operations. The units could be dispatched to Virginia, Delaware, and Pennsylvania. [128] This authorization would be expanded at later date to encompass service in New Jersey and New York.[129] These units would come to be known as the Maryland State Regulars. We'll concentrate on the independent companies and infantry battalion.

[121] Peter Force, ed. *American Archives*: Fifth Series, Volumes I, 2, 3. "A Documentary History of the United States of America from the Declaration of Independence, July 4, 1776 to the Definitive Treaty of Peace with Great Britain, September 3, 1783." Washington: M. St Claire Clarke & Peter Force, 1848. Vol 1. 5.
[122] Force, *Archives*, 4th Ser, Vol. 6. 1258.
[123] Force, *Archives*, 5th Ser, Vol. 1. 15.
[124] Force, *Archives*, 5th Ser, Vol. 1. 31-32.
[125] Ibid. 32.
[126] Ibid. 153-54, 184, 216.
[127] Ibid. 1024.
[128] Maryland Historical Society. *Archives of Maryland : Muster Rolls and Other Records of Service of Maryland Troops in the American Revolution 1775-1783.* (Baltimore: Maryland Historical Society, 1900),Vol 18. 4.
[129] Force, *Archives*, 5th Ser, Vol. 1. 5.

The Independent Maryland Companies were raised from among nine counties (See Table 2). Although ordered to march North as early as July 6th, several of the Independent Companies don't appear in New Jersey until later in August. On July 7th the Council of Safety ordered Captain Edward Veazey's 7th Independent Company to "march immediately to Philadelphia, the service requires the utmost dispatch."[130] Captain Veazey's was the only Independent Company to march with Colonel Smallwood's command. The Colonel mentions in a October 12th report that a "General Return of the Battalion & Veazy's company being all the Troops I march'd from Maryland with..." along with an account of equipment was included in the dispatch.[131] A letter dealing with paying the troops, dated October 18th, reflects that Veazey's Company was to be due pay for Continental service dating from July 6th, the same as Smallwood's Battalion.[132] Captain Edward Veazey was killed in action on Long Island on August 27th, 1776.[133]

Company #	County/ies raised in	Captain Commanding (substitute)
1st	Charles, Calvert	Rezin Beall (1st Lt. Bennet Bracco)
2nd	Somerset	John Gunby
3rd	Worcester	John Watkins
4th	Talbot	James Hindman
5th	St. Mary's	John Allen Thomas
6th	Dorchester	Thomas Woolford
7th	Queen Anne's , Kent	Edward Veazy [Veazey]

Table 2. County allocations for troops serving in the Independent Maryland Companies.
Source: Archives of Maryland Online, vol. 18.

In March, the Council of Safety had ordered Captain John Allen Thomas' 5th Independent Company to be stationed at Leonard Town in St. Mary's County.[134] In July the unit was apparently ordered to march for Philadelphia around the same date as Captain Veazey's command. The 5th Independent first appears to actually be underway northwards in an August 9th correspondence of the Council of Safety. [135] On July 13th the Council had received reports of the appearance of a "considerable number of ships and small vessels" in the Chesapeake Bay. A British fleet had arrived and great concern was felt about a potential invasion being in the making. To defend against this, orders were sent out for the Militia to gather. Included were directives to three of the Independent Companies, the 1st, 4th, and 5th to redirect their units to the area concerned. The Council of Safety's July 15th letter to Capt Thomas of the 5th Company reflects "Sir: We have just received intelligence that makes it necessary for us to stop your proceeding up the bay with your company. We therefore desire that you will immediately return with it to Annapolis."[136]

---

[130] Maryland State Archives. *Archives of Maryland Online: Journals and Correspondence of the Maryland Council of Safety,*(henceforth noted as *Archives of Maryland Online, Journals... Council of Safety),* Vol 12, 5. http://aomol.net/html/index.html, 28 July, 2006.

[131] Ibid, 343.

[132] Ibid, 366.

[133] Rieman Steuart, *A History of the Maryland Line in the Revolutionary War,* (Maryland: Society of the Cincinnati of Maryland, 1969) 6.

[134]*Archives of Maryland Online, Journals... Council of Safety,* Vol. 11. 245.

[135] Force, *Archives,* 5th Ser, Vol. 1. 863.

[136] Ibid. 344.

On July 13th, Captain James Hindman of the 4th Independent Maryland Company wrote to the Council of Safety advising he had begun his march to the "head of *Elk*" in route to Philadelphia.[137] He too received swift orders countermanding his movements. The Council's dispatch to him on July 15th read, "Sir: We have just received intelligence that Lord Dunmore, with the fleet under his command, is in motion about the bay; and as his designs are uncertain, we think it necessary, for the service of the Province, that you, and the company under your command, instead of proceeding up the bay to march to Philadelphia, should directly, with your company, come to Annapolis, where you may receive further orders."[138]

Captain Rezin Beall's 1st Independent Company was stationed in St. Mary's County when the British fleet arrived. The Company was placed under the command of a Colonel Richard Barnes. In a letter to Captain Beall, dated July 15th, The Council instructed that "You will stay in St. Mary's County so long as you apprehend the enemy may have any design of landing there, or making any attempt to distress or plunder the inhabitants."[139] Around the 16th of July the Captain's command apparently fought with enemy forces. A letter from Brigadier General Dent, the commander of the Maryland forces in the area, reflects "on my arrival at this place [Charles River] on the 16th Inst. I found there had been an engagement with the Enemy with no loss but the misfortune of Capt Rezin Beall being badly wounded, tho' its hoped not mortal."[140] The Captain's wounds would prove not to be fatal. However, he would not remain in command of the 1st Independent Company. As noted earlier Rezin Beall was promoted to the rank of Brigadier General "for the flying camp" on August 16th.[141] His previous command would be taken over by his second, Bennet Bracco, promoted by the Maryland Convention to the rank Captain on August 22nd.[142] The Captain was killed in action at White Plains on October 28th.[143] Fate creates strange and twisted circumstances.

Thomas Price wrote from the Upper Camp Prince Georges on July 26th regarding the circumstances then surrounding the presence of the British fleet there.

> The enemy comes on St. George's island in the day time to get water and wood and in the evening retire on board their ships.... There is three pieces of cannon... one a nine pounder one a four the other three I have another on the south west side of the river...a four pounder. I have about four hundred men (half of which is well armed, the other but poorly) placed on each side St. George's River.... I have good reason to think...I can prevent the Enemy's landing or plundering the Inhabitants. I yesterday sent one hundred men on the Island...they lay hid 'till they came from the ships to water, the advanced party being rather eager was too soon discovered and the whole Enemy ran to their boats.... Pursuing them with all speed and firing on them as they were geting into their boats...killed three or four...and several Wounded and one taken prisoner.

[137] Ibid, 252.
[138] Ibid.344.
[139] Ibid. 343.
[140] *Archives of Maryland Online, Journals... Council of Safety,* Vol 12. 83.
[141] Maryland State Archives. *Archives of Maryland Online:Proceedings of the Conventions of the Province of Maryland, 1774-1776,* (henceforth noted as *Archives of Maryland Online, Proceedings...Conventions)* Vol 78. 219. http://www.mdarchives.state.md.us/megafile/msa/speccol/sc2900/sc2908/000001/000078/. 30 May 2006.
[142] Force, *Archives,* 5th Ser, Vol. 3. 93.
[143] Ibid. 487.

...I get from the Prisoners and many deserters that the whole fleet does not intend to stay here longer than those up Potowmack conies down.[144]

By the 30th of July the Council of Safety had concluded that the enemy fleet presented no significant hazard. In correspondence dated August 2nd the Council noted " that the British fleet ...were very weak in land forces, not exceeding three hundred men; that they were so sickly that fifty dead bodies had appeared on shore, chiefly negroes; and that having gone up river ...to take on water [it was] imagined they would soon sail." Their forces appeared so "inconsiderable and comtemptible..." that all the Militia forces were dismissed in St. Mary's County. Orders directing Captain Thomas' 5th Independent Company to resume its march north were issued. Captain Hindman's 4th Independent Company was to be replaced by militia units so it too could proceed to Philadelphia.[145] Later, the four remaining Independent Companies [1st,2nd, 3rd, & 6th] would apparently receive orders to march north. The Return of September 27th (see Figure 1) reflects six of the companies being with Colonel Smallwood in New York. The 3rd Independent Company, commanded by Captain John Watkins does not appear among the listed units.

...Smallwood's Battalion of State Regulars

As noted earlier, the Maryland Convention had directed Colonel Smallwood's command to march for Philadelphia. William Smallwood was born in 1732, a descendent of settlers that arrived in Maryland in 1664. He came from a wealthy planter family. William attended school in England and first saw military service during the French and Indian War. He had served as member of the Maryland Assembly before the Revolution. Commissioned as a Colonel on

14 January 1776, he raised the unit that would gain renown as Smallwood's Maryland Battalion. The Battalion was composed of "men of honor, family and fortune." [146] They would join with the previously mentioned Colonel Haslet's Delaware Regiment as part of Lord Stirling's Brigade. The Maryland Regulars would serve gallantly during the battle on Long Island.

Colonel Smallwood, along with six companies of his battalion, departed Annapolis on July 10th, destined for Philadelphia. The unit initially marched to the head of the Elk River to embark on boats. Major Mordecai Gist, his subordinate, left Baltimore with three additional companies for the same destination. From the Elk River the units

---

[144] . *Archives of Maryland Online, Journals... Council of Safety,* Vol 12. 122-123.
[145] Force, *Archives,* 5th Ser, Vol. 1. 722.
[146] Boatner. 1013.

marched towards Philadelphia.[147] The Philadelphia Committee reported to the Congress on July 16th, "This afternoon the First Battalion of Maryland Regulars, commanded by Colonel Smallwood, arrived in this city, on their way to the *Jerseys*, where they are to compose a part of the Flying Camp."[148] Upon his arrival in the city, Colonel Smallwood presented himself to the Congress and awaited further orders.

On July 17th John Hancock informed Colonel Smallwood, " Sir: I have it in charge from Congress to direct you, as soon as possible, march the troops from *Maryland*, now in this city, to New York, and there put yourself under the command of General Washington. The exigency of the service requiring as speedy a junction as possible of your troops with those at *New York*. I recommend you use all dispatch in your power."[149] Unexplainably another letter from John Hancock to General Washington of the same date appears to give different orders to Smallwood's Battalion. He writes to General Washington, "upwards of a thousand troops from *Maryland* are now in this city, on their way to join the Flying Camp in *New-Jersey*. They are an exceeding fine body of men, will begin their march this day."[150] Where the change in orders from New York to New Jersey occurred is uncertain. The Maryland Regulars would have a short association with the Flying Camp.

By July 25th the Marylanders had passed through Woodbridge, New Jersey. On July 26th Colonel Smallwood received orders from General Mercer to halt his march and remain at Elizabethtown. The General, in an August 4th letter to John Hancock, reported that "Colonel *Smallwood's* battalion, from *Maryland*, remains at *Elizabeth-Town*, but expect daily to have orders to proceed to *New York*."[151] Those orders were received when General Washington directed General Mercer to send forward two-thousand troops from the Flying Camp. The Commander in Chief explains to John Hancock in an August 9th letter, "I have written to General *Mercer* for two thousand men from the Flying Camp. Colonel *Smallwood's* battalion, as a part of them I expect this forenoon."[152] The Regiment was in New York by August 12th as General Washington notes in a letter of that date to John Hancock. On September 27th, Colonel Smallwood submitted a Return showing the all of the Maryland units assigned and then with his command (see Figure 1).

---

[147] J Thomas Scharf. *History of Maryland from the Earliest Period to the Present Day,* (Baltimore: Piet, 1879), 240.
[148] Force, *Archives,* 5th Ser, Vol. 1. 350.
[149] Ibid. 388.
[150] Ibid. 387.
[151] Ibid. 750.
[152] Ibid. 835.

COMPANIES.	Colonel.	Lieut. Colonel.	Majors.	Captains.	First Lieutenants.	Second Lieut'ms.	Third Lieut'nts.	Ensigns.	Chaplains.	Paymasters.	Adjutant.	Quartermaster.	Surgeons.	Mates.	Sergeants.	Drums and Fifes.	Present, fit for duty.	Sick, present.	Sick, absent.	On command.	On furlough.	Total.	Sergeants.	Drums and Fifes.	Privates.	Inlisted.	Dead.	Discharged.	Deserted.
Captain Gunby	-	-	-	1	-	2	-	-	-	-	-	-	-	-	4	2	44	19	12	6	-	81	-	-	15	-	1	-	-
Captain Hindman	-	-	-	1	1	1	1	-	-	-	-	-	-	-	3	1	54	26	3	6	-	89	-	-	7	-	-	-	-
Captain Thomas	-	-	1	1	1	1	-	-	-	-	-	-	-	-	3	-	56	10	22	6	-	94	-	2	2	-	1	-	1
Captain Woolford	-	-	1	-	1	-	-	-	-	-	-	-	-	-	2	1	46	24	19	7	-	96	-	1	-	-	-	-	-
Captain Bracco	-	-	1	-	1	-	-	-	-	-	-	-	-	-	1	2	16	16	55	7	-	94	-	-	2	-	-	-	-
Late Captain Veazey	-	-	1	-	-	-	-	-	-	-	-	-	-	-	2	1	12	-	17	3	-	32	1	1	64	-	-	-	-
Captain Stone	-	-	1	1	-	-	-	-	-	-	-	-	-	-	4	1	36	-	14	6	-	56	-	1	8	-	-	-	-
Captain Lucas	-	-	1	-	-	1	-	-	-	-	-	-	-	-	4	1	36	-	4	3	-	23	-	1	41	-	-	-	-
Captain Ramsey	-	-	1	-	1	-	-	-	-	-	-	-	-	-	2	1	21	4	24	7	-	56	-	1	8	-	-	-	-
Captain Adams	-	-	-	-	-	-	-	-	-	-	-	-	-	-	3	2	9	2	-	6	-	4	2	49	-	-	-	-
Captain Scott	-	-	1	1	1	-	-	-	-	-	-	-	-	-	4	1	29	2	19	7	-	57	-	1	7	-	-	-	-
Captain Smith	-	-	1	1	1	1	-	-	-	-	-	-	-	-	3	1	33	-	16	7	-	56	1	1	8	1	-	-	1
Captain Sym	-	-	1	1	1	1	-	-	-	-	-	-	-	-	4	1	34	5	9	7	-	55	-	1	8	-	-	-	-
Captain Bowie	-	-	-	-	-	-	-	-	-	-	-	-	-	-	1	1	4	2	4	2	-	12	3	1	52	-	-	-	-
Captain Ford	-	-	-	-	1	-	-	-	-	-	-	-	-	-	1	2	15	-	10	4	-	29	3	-	39	-	-	-	-
Total	1	1	1	8	6	10	4	3	-	1	1	1	-	2	38	16	419	116	237	80	-	846	12	12	310	1	2	-	2

W. SMALLWOOD.

Captain *Gunby's* Second and Third Lieutenant sick.
Captain *Hindman*, on command to *Philadelphia*, to procure clothes for his Company: his First Lieutenant and Sergeant sick.
Captain *Woolford*, his First and Second Lieutenants and two Sergeants sick.
Captain *Bracco's* First and Third Lieutenants and three Sergeants sick.
Late Captain *Veazey's* Sergeant on command.
Captain *Stone* sick.
Captain *Lucas*, sick.
Captain *Ramsey's* Lieutenant and Ensign sick; two Sergeants also.
Captain *Adams* and his First Lieutenant sick.
Captain *Scott's* Ensign sick.
Captain *Smith's* Drummer deserted.
Captain *Ford* and his First Lieutenant sick.

Barbers and Camp-Colour Men 28
Attending the Sick...............................12
Waiters on Field, Staff, and Commissioned Officers....40

Total..80

Captain *Stone*, in his last week's return, returned one of his Sergeants as Sergeant Major, and a man wanting in his place; he having returned to his former station, makes one more.
Captain *Adams* finds four men in the Hospital, thought to have been lost at *Long-Island.*
Captain *Ramsey*, four men this week more than last, owing to his four Corporals having been left out of his last week's return.

Figure 1, Force, *Archives,* 5th Ser, Vol. 2. 568.

Maryland Flying Camp

Tasked to provide 3400 troops for the Flying Camp, the dispatch of the Colonel Smallwood's command was considered to have filled a portion of that quota, 1384 troops. The remaining rank and file was to be volunteers raised from among the State militia. The Maryland Flying Camp was to be composed of four battalions plus one company. Each battalion was to consist of nine companies, with each having 90 members. This organization would have provided 3330 troops plus the command and staff for a total of 3405 officers and soldiers.

On August 9th the Maryland Council of Safety wrote to the State's delegates in Philadelphia. Their correspondence included details about the efforts towards reaching their Flying Camp quota. Among the units mentioned was Captain Jacob Good's Company[153][154] from Frederick, which was already underway. Orders directing the remainder of Colonel Charles Greenbury Griffith's Frederick battalion to proceed to Philadelphia were issued on August 7th.[155][156] Captain Peter Mantz' company, of the

---

[153] Henry C Peden. *Revolutionary Patriots of Frederick County, Maryland 1775-1783.* Westminster MD: Willow Bend Books, 2000. Jacob Good of Frederick County was a patriot and soldier. He served as a militia officer starting in 1775. He was appointed a Captain in the Maryland Flying Camp and started raising his company in July 1776.
[154] *Archives of Maryland : Muster Rolls ...,* 46. Roster of Captain Jacob Good's Flying Camp Company.
[155] *Archives of Maryland Online, Journals... Council of Safety,* Vol 12, 179.

Frederick battalion, had been ordered to proceed to St. Mary's to "take the place" of Captain Thomas' 5th Independent Company.[157] Captain Mantz' unit was later redirected to march north to Philadelphia, arriving there on August 23rd.[158] From Colonel Thomas Ewing's battalion three companies were preparing to march. The lack of weapons and supplies for the battalion was delaying the march of the full unit. It was proposed that Colonel Carvell Hall's battalion of 810 men would be retained in Maryland. The Council noted that two or three East Shore companies would be ready to march the following week. Two additional companies were obtaining arms and were to replace the independent companies of Captains Edward Veazey and James Hindman, sent earlier. The Council noted the difficulties of raising the units, "Under all these difficulties, arising from the want of arms and necessaries, and also from the resignations, we are exerting ourselves to the utmost. Money has flowed out of the Treasury very freely upon this important occasion. We hope for the approbation of the honorable Congress and Convention." [159]

Thomas Stone, a Maryland delegate to the Congress, replied to the Maryland Council of Safety on August 13th. His letter presents an excellent example of encouragement and support given to those striving to raise the Maryland Flying Camp.

Gentlemen: I am very glad to be informed that Lord *Dunmore* and his fleet have quitted the Bay, and am hopeful this circumstance will induce your Militia to lend assistance to their neighbors with more alacrity than could have been expected while an enemy was hovering on their coast. You may be assured they are much wanted in the *Jerseys* and at *New-York*, where an attack is daily expected, and at both which places our strength is by no means sufficient to oppose the enemy with the certainty of success which every man who considers the importance of the event must wish.

Captain *Thomas* is arrived with his company. I shall rejoice to see Colonel *Griffith* with his troops, and shall with pleasure afford him and all other officers and troops from *Maryland* any assistance in my power. I shall show particular attention to Colonel *Griffith*, your recommendation entitling him to particular notice.

The difficulties you have experienced in raising your quota of the Flying Camp I am convinced have been distressing; but I hope they are now pretty well over. You may have any money you want from Congress, upon application. The enemy's strength at *Staten-Island* is fifteen thousand men. The *Hessians* are daily expected: by the last accounts, they were shipping their men, and making all necessary preparations for an attack. General *Washington* is not so strong as he could wish. Upon these movements of the enemy, he ordered a reinforcement of two thousand from *Jersey* to *York*. The *Maryland* battalion was immediately sent to him; but I believe the camps in *Jersey* were too weak to spare any more. I observe many of the Militia of this State [Pennsylvania] in

---

[156] Peden. 149. Charles Greenbury Griffith was a Frederick County patriot and soldier. On July 30, 1776 "he was appointed colonel of the Battalion of Militia to be raised in Frederick County for the Flying camp…(Archives of Maryland, volume 16)."

[157] *Archives of Maryland Online: Journals … Council of Safety*, Vol 12, 142. June 9, 2006.

[158] . *Archives of Maryland : Muster Rolls …*, 48.

[159] Force, *Archives*, 5th Ser, Vol. 1. 863.

motion; but many are leaving the camp, and are not to be kept there by threats or persuasions. I intend to leave this city on this day week, till which I shall be ready to execute your orders; being, gentlemen, your most obedient servant. T. Stone. [160]

The Council of Safety responded in a letter dated August 16[th:]
We received yours of the 13th.... In consequence of a resolve of the Convention, we have given orders to all the Independent Companies (four in number) to march. Colonel *Carvell Hall's,* and Colonel *Ewing's,* and six or seven companies on the *Eastern-Shore,* have like orders to march; so that, with *Griffith's* battalion, we shall have near four thousand men with you in a short time. This exceeds our proportion for the Flying Camp, but we are sending all that we have that can be armed and equipped; and the people of *New-York,* for whom we have great affection, can have no more than our all. ...We depend, in case of invasion, on being supported powerfully by our neighbors in *Pennsylvania, New-York,* and the *Jerseys,* besides having a part of our own troops sent back"[161] (see Table 3).

Smallwood's Battalion, nine companies, 76 each-	684
Captain Veazey 100, Captain Hindman 100, Captain Thomas 100,	300
Captain Beall 100, Captain Gunby 100,	200
Captain Woolford 100, Captain Watkins 100,	200
Total	1384
[Colonel] Griffith's Battalion, nine companies, 90 men each-	810
Colonel Carvel Hall's Battalion, nine companies, 90 men each	810
Colonel Ewing's Battalion of three companies	270
Eastern-Shore Battalion of seven companies	644
Total	3918

Table 3: "List of Troops for Maryland" (Force. Archive, Vol. 5, Ser1, page 976)

The four remaining companies were eventually provided with the arms and equipment they needed. On August 15th they received their orders to march to the Flying Camp.[162] The Maryland units proceeded to assemble under General Mercer. The Flying Camp return of July 25th listed a total of 3,092 troops, none from Maryland. [163] In a return dated August 20th General Mercer reports 5398 troops on hand. He adds that "There are four companies of *Maryland* inlisted Militia just come in that are not in the returns." [164]

---

[160] Ibid. 930.
[161] Ibid. 975.
[162] Scharf. 242.
[163] Force, *Archives*, 5th Ser, Vol. 1. 556.
[164] Ibid. 1080.

MAJOR GIST.

On August 22nd the British assaulted Long Island, landing at Denyse's Point. Colonel Smallwood's Maryland Battalion, under the command of Major Mordecai Gist, displayed conspicuous gallantry during the ensuing battle on August 27th. Colonel Smallwood had been away to New York, serving at a court-martial. Hurriedly returning to Long Island he was given command over a Connecticut Regiment and the recently arrived 5th Maryland Independent Company. With his ad hoc command he engaged the enemy in minor action and aided beleaguered survivors in retreating across the island's swamps. [165]

After the battle General Washington withdrew his forces to form new defenses below Fort Washington. The General wrote to Congress on September 2nd in what must be one of his most distressed periods:

> Sir: As my intelligence of late has been rather unfavorable and would be viewed with anxiety and concern, peculiarly happy should I esteem myself were it in my power at this time to transmit such information to Congress as would be more pleasing and agreeable to their wishes; but unfortunately for me – unfortunately for them, it is not.
>
> Our situation is truly distressing. The check our detachment sustained on the 27th ultimo has dispirited too great a proportion of our troops, and filed their minds with apprehension and despair. The Militia, instead of calling forth their utmost efforts to a brave and manly opposition in order to repair our losses, &c., are dismayed, intractable, and impatient to return. Great numbers of them have gone off, in some instances almost by whole regiments, half ones, and by companies at a time. .....I am obliged to confess my want of confidence with the generality of the troops. All these circumstances fully confirm the opinion I ever entertained, and which I more than once in my letters took liberty of mentioning to Congress, that no dependence can be put in a Militia or other troops than those enlisted and embodied for a longer period than our regulations heretofore have prescribed. I am persuaded, and as fully convinced as I am of any one fact that has happened, that our liberties must of necessity be greatly hazarded, if not entirely lost, if their defense is left to any but a permanent standing army. I mean one to exist during the war. ... Our number of men present fit for duty, are under twenty thousand. ...I have ordered General *Mercer* to send the men intended for the Flying Camp to this place, about one thousand in number. Till of late,

---

[165] . Scarf. 248.

I had no doubt in my own mind of defending this place, nor should I have yet if the men would do their duty; but this I despair of. Every power I possess shall be exerted to serve the cause, and my first wish is, that whatever may be the event, the Congress will do me the justice to think so. ...[166]

Bitterly disappointed in the Militia, the General despaired over his ability to protect New York. His army had faced an enemy superior in number, materiel, and ability. Farmers, shopkeepers, laborers, and gentlemen had faced the most professional and powerful army then existing. Appreciating the General's concerns, we should consider the opposing forces. Did he underestimate the role and contributions of the citizen soldiers upon the field? He was correct about the need for a more standardized, trained, and experienced regular army to continue the fight for the cause of liberty. The Marylanders already upon the field and those advancing towards the fight would help form the core of that army.

The need for reinforcements in New York was paramount. On September 7th General Mercer advised his Commander-In-Chief that he "gave general orders at all the posts along the *Jersey* shore that the troops from *Maryland* should proceed to *New-York.*" [167] In Maryland, companies under Captains Forrest and Bourke were ordered to march to Annapolis on their way to the Flying Camp. Colonel Smallwood's command retreated with Washington's Army towards White Plains. There on October 28th the Marylanders engaged the British in battle at Chatterton's Hill on the right of the American line. Smallwood's unit first attacked the German mercenary troops (Hessians) who had stopped to build a bridge over the Bronx River at the base of the Hill. The battle continued until around 5 o'clock that evening, leaving the British commanding the battlefield as the Americans withdrew. General Howe regrouped his Army for an assault on the 31st but was delayed by heavy storms. When they advanced on November 1st it was found that General Washington had withdrawn north to a stronger position. [168]

Mordecai Gist, promoted to Colonel, reported on the events to the Maryland Council of Safety in a letter dated November 2nd.

Gentlemen: Colonel Smallwood being wounded in the action of the 28th, ultimo, the command since has devolved upon myself.... Since the skirmish the enemy has been exceedingly busy in erecting a breastwork on the eminence [Chatterton's Hill] they took from us. Yesterday morning, having got prepared to open it upon us, the General ordered us to abandon our back lines.... The enemy immediately took possession of them... and advanced upon us with a large column... the artillery on each side keeping up a smart fire; and they soon found their situation disagreeable, and as if ashamed of the attempt, they sneakingly skulked behind a wood, and retired unseen to the lines.[169]

Doctor John Pine provides in a letter dated November 7th that "Colonel Smallwood's battalion suffered a good deal, the Col. himself wounded in two places, the number of killed and wounded, as the report is in the Camp, ...about 90, but from the

---

[166]. Force, *Archives*, 5th Ser, Vol. 2. 120-121.
[167] Ibid. 212.
[168] Boatner, 1200-1201.
[169] Force, *Archives* 5th Ser, Vol. 3. 486 - 487.

wounded I saw myself in hospital, and adjacent houses, there must at least be an hundred and twenty or thirty wounded the number killed I don't know…. The Enemy went off from this night before last, it is conjectured they are to attack Fort Washington….[170]

Conjectures about General Howe's move upon Fort Washington were correct. The British attacked the bastion on November 16th. Among the defenders were several Maryland units. Correspondence dated November 22nd reflects the loss of "Colonel Rawlings, Col Williams and about 200 of that battalion are prisoners." Also mentioned "of General Beall's Brigade, [Maryland Flying Camp] 160 are prisoners, and Capt. Longs company, he being sick in the Jerseys. Captain Hardman of Fred [Frederick County] and his Company are prisoners. In all the Troops raised in our State above 400 are prisoners."[171]

The battalion identified as "Colonel Rawlings'" was a Maryland /Virginia Rifle Battalion organized under the command of a Colonel Hugh Stephenson in June 1776. Moses Rawlings had been appointed Lieutenant (Lt.) Colonel of the unit. Otho Holland Williams was assigned as Major of the battalion.[172] By November, Colonel Stephenson had perished,[173] Colonel Rawlings commanded and then Lt. Colonel Williams served as second in command. Colonel Rawlings was reported as having been wounded "slightly in the small of the leg" when captured.[174] Moses Rawlings appears to either have been exchanged or had escaped by October 1778. He is found at that time being directed by the Continental Congress to recruit a regiment for service.[175] Lt. Colonel Williams had been wounded "slightly in the upper part of the thigh" during the battle.[176] Held prisoner in New York he was exchanged in January 1778. He assumed command of the new 6th Maryland Regiment but served primarily as a staff officer in the later Southern Campaigns under Horatio Gates and Nathanael Green.[177] Otho Holland Williams originally joined a company of riflemen raised in Maryland in June 1775, commanded by a Captain Thomas Price. Lieutenant Williams served under Washington at the battles around Boston.[178]

The wayward 3rd Maryland Independent Company, under Captain John Watkins command, appears in the above correspondence as Captain Long's Company. As previously noted the 3rd Independent did not appear on Colonel Smallwood's Return dated September 27th. The new commander is Captain Solomon Long, formerly a Second Lieutenant in the Company. He had been commissioned into the unit on January 5th, 1776. He was promoted to the rank of Captain by October that year.[179] It appears that Captain Watkins may have been dismissed from his command. A letter of September 30th from Thomas Stone, the Maryland Congressional delegate in Philadelphia, to the

---

[170] *Archives of Maryland Online: Journals … Council of Safety,* Vol 12, 480. March 1, 2004.
[171] Ibid. 473.
[172] Maryland State Archives. *Archives of Maryland Online, Muster Rolls and Other Records of Service of Maryland Troops in the American Revolution 1775-1783. ,*(henceforth noted as *Archives of Maryland Online: Muster Rolls…) * Vol 18, 77. www.mdarchives.state.md.us…26 October 2006.
[173] L. Edward Purcell. *Who Was Who in the American Revolution.* (New York: Facts on File, 1993), 512.
[174] Force, *Archives* 5th Ser, Vol. 3. 730.
[175] *Archives of Maryland Online,, Muster Rolls…..* Vol 18. 77.
[176] Force, *Archives* 5th Ser, Vol. 3. 730.
[177] Purcell. *Who Was Who in the American Revolution.* 512.
[178]. Colonel J. Thomas Scarf. "Gen. Otho Holland Williams: Memoir of His Life and Services" *Pamphlets in American History.* "Miscellany of Revolutionary War Biographies." Group 1, (microform).(Sanford, NC:Microfilming Corporation of America,1979. No. B/RW 128.
[179] Henry C Peden, Jr. *Revolutionary Patriots of Worcester & Somerset Counties, Maryland 1775-1783.* (Westminster MD: Willow Bend Books,2000).182-183.

Maryland Council of Safety speaks poorly of Captain Watkins. It reads in part "Capt Watkins did not leave the City as soon as I expected he would do. I fear nothing will do with him but dismission."[180] The assumption of the Company's command by Solomon Long appears to support Watkins removal. Solomon Long was not with his Company at Fort Washington, being sick at the time. He would recover and continue to serve, reaching the rank of Lt. Colonel in 1782.[181]

The Frederick County unit mentioned above was the Company of Captain Henry Hardman. The unit was raised in July 1776, in the "Frederick County- Upper District", now Washington County. It was assigned to the First Battalion of the Maryland Flying Camp. Henry Hardman was among exchanged prisoners of war returning in August 1778.[182]

Maryland continued to reinforce the Flying Camp, raising additional companies through September and into October.[183] In the field the troops had fallen upon meager times. The repeated reversals on the field of battle must have been demoralizing. The ability to supply the troops with essentials was stretched to the breaking point. An example is found in a letter from Captain Hindman of the 4th Independent Company, dated October 12th. " He had gone to Philadelphia four days prior "in search of necessary cloathing for the Maryland Regular troops, am much afraid shall not be able to procure... particularly shoes and stockings, of which we are in great want....[And] unless they can be got will render many soldiers unfit for duty.... I can assure you the very thoughts of keeping our troops at Camp all winter disheartens them very much." He relates that these burdens were increased by the "severe duty and great fatigue they [the Maryland troops] have undergone ...." Captain Hindman reflects that sufficient provisions existed but were restricted to "a constant succession of beef and flour" with a lack of salt and "no kind of vegetables" being furnished.[184]

On October 9th the Maryland Convention met to discuss the quota placed upon the State to raise troops for the new Continental Army. It was decided to engage as many members of the existing Regular State Troops and the Flying-Camp Militia as possible to serve in the eight new battalions. The Convention resolved "That the Officers to whom warrants issued for the enrollment of Non-Commissioner Officers and Privates for the two last Battalions...to be raised for the Flying-Camp, immediately return lists of men by them enrolled...and forbear any further enrollment; that...Companies as are full or nearly full, be equipped and marched as soon as may be,...Companies as are not nearly full be discharged...."[185] No further efforts would be made to reinforce the Maryland Flying Camp.

The term of service for those in the Flying Camp would expire at the beginning of December. There were efforts afoot to retain as many of the troops already serving. In the Continental Congress, on December 3rd, it was resolved to "...settle with and pay the Militia of the *Maryland* Flying-Camp. That ...Rations, in lieu of mileage" be provided to those Maryland soldiers who chose to return home. Those Non-Commissioned Officers and soldiers who enlisted for the next three years were to be clothed immediately. Those of the Maryland militia who had agreed to remain for one additional month wee to "be

---

[180] *Archives of Maryland Online: Journals ... Council of Safety,* Vol 12. 311.
[181] Peden,183.
[182] *Archives of Maryland Online: Muster Rolls...,* Vol 18. 48, 616.
[183] Force, *Archives* 5th Ser, Vol. 3. 625-644.
[184] *Archives of Maryland Online: Journals ... Council of Safety,* Vol 12. 344-345.
[185] Force, *Archives* 5th Ser, Vol. 3. 121.

supplied...with a shirt, a pair of Shoes, and a pair of Stockings.... The militia that had agreed to stay in service until March 10th, 1777 was to be given shoes, stockings, rations, and pay as the "troops on the Continental establishment" along with one month's advanced pay. Finally, the Congress resolved "That the Officers of the *Maryland* Troops be requested immediately to parade those Troops, and use their utmost influence to persuade their adoption of the terms proposed by Congress" to enlist into the Continental Army.[186]

The Maryland contingents to the Flying Camp fought in the battles at Long Island, Harlem Plains and Harlem Heights, White Plains, and Fort Washington. No State can be said to have donated more for the cause of liberty; in men, treasure, and blood; than did Maryland.

---

[186] Ibid. 1597-98.

Chapter 5
Pennsylvania

"Where brave men fought the foe of freedom..."[187]

Pennsylvania would eventually take the leading role in supplying manpower and materiel for the Flying Camp. First, the Pennsylvanians had to overcome a series of obstructions to enable them to march forth to the defense of their new nation.

Two revolutions effectively occurred in Pennsylvania during that pivotal year. Both of which would directly impact the conduct of the war. One revolt was against the British Crown, the other struck the established provincial powers. Pennsylvanians held deep differences of opinion regarding the rebellion, ranging from fanatical support, to grudging acceptance, through distinct opposition. In the decade preceding the Revolution most were generally opposed to British trade and tax policies. Still, the rising tide of opposition in the colony didn't draw all citizens to the cause. Other concerns overshadowed many personal and political views of the relationship with Britain. The apex to which these concerns would rise was the provincial Assembly. [188]

For decades the Assembly was dominated by the founding Quakers. They and their supporters held strong pacifist views. Under their control the Colony didn't pursue substantial or sustained efforts regarding military affairs. As a result, Pennsylvania lagged behind in military preparedness compared to its neighboring States. The militia law had been allowed to expire without replacement. Leaving no official obligation upon the inhabitants to form or provide for militia units. Several groups formed during the French and Indian War and the Paxton Boy's revolt did continue to exist. These were insufficient in numbers and left Pennsylvania ill prepared to provide the troops needed in the looming conflict. [189]

The battles at Lexington and Concord awoke the people, who then arose to take action. Many of its citizens, including Loyalist, Quakers, and others were "stunned by the unexpected events in Massachusetts." [190] Many changed their views regarding the brewing rebellion. John Adams commented to his wife in a letter of June 2nd that "Dr. Warren writes me.... He would burst to see whole Companies of armed Quakers in this City, in Uniforms, going thro the Manual and Maneuvres like regular Troops." [191]

The lack of an official means for establishing the militia prompted the authorities in several counties and Philadelphia to create volunteer units. The Northampton and Bucks Counties committees strove to have their citizens "to form themselves into Associations[192]... to improve themselves in the military art." The Chester County

---

[187] Eddie Khoury, Ronnie Banner. *Pennsylvania.* (1989). www. netstate.com/state/symb/song/pa-pa. 8 August 2005.

[188] Anne M Ousterhout. *A State Divided: Opposition in Pennsylvania to the American Revolution.* (New York: Greenwood Press, 1987). 1.

[189] Samuel Newland, *The Pennsylvania Militia: The Early Years 1669-1792,* (Anneville, PA: Pennsylvania National Guard Association, 1997), 125.

[190] Ousterhout. 103.

[191] Letter from John Adams to Abigail Adams, 2 June 1775 [electronic edition]. *Adams Family Papers: An Electronic Archive.* Massachusetts Historical Society. http://www.masshist.org/digitaladams/

[192] Regarding Pennsylvania units the terms militia, assoications, and associators are frequently used interchangebly. For a better understanding of the organization of units during the period I refer you to Newland's: *The Pennsylvania Militia: The Early Years 1669-1792* and Trussell 's *The Pennsylvania Line: Regimental Organization and Operations, 1776-1783.*

committee met in May and called for military association, adopting a measure already used in other parts of the colony. The volunteers had to agree to learn military art, obey their officers, support civil authorities and be prepared to defend their country. Those joining the volunteer units would come to be known as Associators.[193]

Raising these quasi-official armed units further complicated the already confusing issue of leadership in Pennsylvania. Adding to such, the provincial Assembly had been called upon to form an "administrative agency to coordinate defense and act in an emergency. " The Pennsylvania Committee of Safety was created, the establishment of which effectively resulted in Pennsylvania being "ruled by two different systems." [194] The difficulties of having a split and contentious system of government impeded efforts to raise forces against the gathering storm of war.

On June 3rd the Continental Congress tasked Pennsylvania to provide the bulk of the Flying Camp's forces. It "*Resolved,* That the colony of Pennsylvania be requested to furnish of the militia, 6000." [195] The fractured state of government in the Colony seriously hindered raising this force. The Assembly's efforts floundered. On June 14th it was "*Resolved,* By the members of assembly now met, that they are earnestly desirous of carrying into execution the resolutions of congress 1st inst, but that as they despair after repeated disappointments of procuring a quorum of the house, they find themselves unable at this time to proceed on said resolutions."[196] The Assembly's failure to act prompted the Committee of Safety, on June 19th, to order "That the Delegates of the Province in Congress be requested to inform Congress that their recommendation relative to forming the Flying Camp was not carried into execution by the Assembly, and desire to be informed whether it is their intention that this Board should take upon them the execution of the same."[197]

The following day Robert Morris, a Pennsylvania delegate, "reminded the Congress that the Assembly of said Province had adjourned on the 14th instant, without having been able to carry into execution the said resolves of the Congress of the 3d instant for raising six thousand Militia for establishing the Flying Camp." Mister Morris noted that the original resolves left the Committee of Safety in doubt as to what steps should be taken. The Committee desired to know if "it would be expected from them to execute the said Resolve, as they are in recess of Assembly the Executive body of this Province."[198] They wanted Congress' express direction to act so an appearance of authority would exist. Congress debated the issue and several motions were presented. The vote went against any action or direction being given to the Committee of Safety.

Congressional reluctance to intercede in the boiling political caldron of Pennsylvania politics left the issue of the Flying Camp simmering. Meanwhile, the political initiative would pass to yet another competing group. On June 18th "a number of gentlemen met at Carpenter's Hall, in Philadelphia, being deputed by the committees of

---

[193] Ousterhout. 104-105.
[194] Ibid. 106-107.
[195] Peter Force, ed., ", *A Documentary History of the English Colonies in North America from the King's Message to Parliament of March 7,1774 to the Declaration of Independence of the United States.* American Archives: Fourth Series, volume VI. (Hereafter known as Force, *Archives* 4th Ser, Vol. 6)(Washington: M. St. Claire Clarke and Peter Force, 1846), Report of the Continental Congress, May 24, 1776. 1696
[196] *Journals of the House of Representatives of the Commonwealth of Pennsylvania.* Vol.1. (Philadelphia: John Dunlap, 1782), 42. (Henceforth :*Journals...Pennsylvania*)
[197] Force, *Archives* 4th Ser, Vol. 6. 1286.
[198] Ibid, 1288.

several counties of the province, to join in provincial conference." The conference was convened in response to a Congressional resolution that recommended the "total suppression of all authority under the king of Great-Britain." It was "recommended to the respective assemblies and conventions, of the united colonies, where no government sufficient to the exigencies of their affairs has been hitherto established to adopt such government as shall in the opinion of the representatives of the people, best conduce to the happiness and safety of their constituents in particular, and America in general." The resolution was "fully approved" by the Conference. Members also decided "the present government of this province is not competent to the exigencies of our affairs." It was declared "That it is necessary that a provincial convention be called by this conference for the express purpose of forming a new government in this province, on the authority of the people."[199] That motion set the stage for the overthrow of the colonial government and the existing Assembly.

This Conference of Committees devoted their time to arranging the election of convention members and the issuance of relevant proclamations. On June 23rd a review was conducted of the events surrounding attempts to establish the Flying Camp. It was declared that as the Assembly and the Committee of Safety had failed to establish the Flying Camp it fell to the Conference to act. It was resolved "That this conference do recommend to the committees and associators of this province, to embody 4500 of the militia, which with 1500 men now in the pay of this province, will be the quota of this colony required by congress." A committee was delegated to "devise ways and means for raising the said 4500 men, and to enquire into all means necessary to fit them for taking the field."[200] On the same day the "Deputies from the Committees of Pennsylvania" issued a proclamation to the citizenry proclaiming; "*Friends and Countrymen*, In obedience to the power we derived from you, we have fixed upon a mode of electing a convention to form a government for the province of Pennsylvania, under the *authority of the people*."[201] Thus, the die was cast and a rebellion against the established provincial hierarchy was underway.

On June 25th the Conference established a committee of three to draft an "address to the associators of this province, on the subject of embodying 4500 men." The previously appointed Ways and Means Committee made its report to the Conference. The Conference "*Resolved unanimously,* That it be recommended to the Associators of the city of Philadelphia, and several counties, to embody themselves."[202]

---

[199] *Journals...Pennsylvania.* 34-36.
[200] Ibid, 42.
[201] Ibid, 44

[202] Ibid.

The proportions assigned to the different Associations are reflected in Table 4.

City of Philadelphia	210
County of Philadelphia	740
" " Bucks	400
" " Chester	652
" " Lancaster	746
" " Berks	666
" " Northampton	346
" " York	400
" " Cumberland	334
Colonel Miles Troops	1500

Table 4. Pennsylvania Association Proportions. Journals...Pennsylvania.44

In total, 6000 troops were to be provided by the province. It was directed that the:

> "4500 militia to be raised, be formed into six battalions; each battalion to be commanded by one colonel, one lieutenant-colonel, one major; the staff to consist of a chaplain, a surgeon, an adjutant, a quarter-master, and a surgeon's mate; and to have one sergeant-major, one quarter-master sergeant, a drum-major, and a fife-major; and to be composed of nine companies, viz eight battalion companies , to consist of a captain, two lieutenants, and one ensign, four sergeants, four corporals, a drummer, a fifer, and fifty-six privates each; and one rifle company to consist of a captain, three lieutenants, four sergeants, four corporals, one drummer, one fifer, and eighty privates; excepting for the Chester county battalion; one company of artillery is to be raised in the city of Philadelphia, instead of a rifle company. " [203]

The Committee preparing the Associators Address presented its draft. It was twice read aloud and then unanimously approved.

"The A D D R E S S of the Deputies of the Committees of Pennſylvania,
affembled in Provincial
Conference; at Philadelphia. June 25, 1776.

To THE ASSOCI ATORS of P E N NSYLVANIA.

GENTLE MEN ,~
THE only defign of our meeting together was to put an end to our *own* power in the province,by fixing upon a plan for calling a convention to form a government under the authority of the people. But the fudden and unexpected feperation of the late affèmblv, has compelled us to under—take the execution of a refolve of congrefs, for calling forth 4500 of the militia of the province to join the militia of the neighbouring colonies, to form a camp for our immediate protection. We perfume only to *recommend* the plan we have formed to you, trufting that in cafe of fo much confequence your love of virtue, and zeal for liberty will fupply the

---

[203] Ibid.

want of authority delegated to us expreffly for that purpofe.

We need not remind you that you are *now* furnifhed with new motives to animate and fupportt your courage. You are not about to contend against the power of Great-Brirain in order to difplace one fet of villians, to make room for another. Your arms will not he enervated in the day of battle, with the reflection that you are to rifk your lives, or fhed your blood for a British tyrant, or that your pofterity will have your work to do over again.---You are about to contend for *permanent* freedom, to be fupported by a government which will be derived from yourfelves,. and which will have for its object not the emolument of one man, or clafs of men only, but the fafety, liberty, and happinefs of every indvidual in the community.

We call upon you therefore by the refpect and obedience which are due to the authority of the united colonics, to concur in this important meafure. The prefent campaign will probably decide the fate of America. It is now in your power to immortalize your names, by mingling your atchievements with the events of the year 1776---a year which we hope will be famed in the annals of hiftory to the end of time, for eftablifhing upon a lafting foundation the liberties of one quarter of the globe.

Remember the honor of our colony is at ftake. Should you defert the common caufe at: the prefent juncture, the glory you have acquired by your former exertions of ftrength and virtue will be tamifhed, and our friends and brethren, who are now acquiring laurels in the moft remote parts of America will reproach us, and blufh to own themfelves natives or- inhabitants of Pennfylvania.

But there are other motives before you——your houfes——your fields, the legacies of your anceftors, or the dear bought fruits of your own induftry, and your liberty, now urge you to the field. These can not plead with you in vain, or we might point out to you further, your wives, your children, your aged fathers and mothers, who now look up to you for aid, and hope for falvation in this day of calamity only from the inftrumentality of your fwords.

Signed by an unanimous Order of the Conference

T H O M A S M'K E A N, Prefident" .

With this concluding act the members thanked their President for his services and the City of Philadelphia for its "unwearied endeavours in the public fervice." [204] The Conference was dissolved at the end of the day on June 25th. Regarding the Pennsylvania Flying Camp, the Conference accomplished more, in a shorter period of time, than the Assembly or the Committee of Safety would or could possibly have achieved. The political storm raging across the province abated with the actions of the Conference. The call-to-arms had been sent forth to the Associations. In a July 4th letter to General Washington, John Hancock reflected on the struggle "for possession of Power" in the province and the impact of events on raising the Flying Camp. He commented that "unhappy confusions…. prevailed" in Pennsylvania and could "principally be ascribed the delay" regards the Flying Camp. Hancock wrote that "things will now take a different turn" and a "new model of government" agreeable to the Congress would be established.[205]

---

[204] Ibid.45-46.
[205] Force, *Archives* 4th Ser, Vol. 6. 1258.

Flag of Hanover Associators-1775. Pennsylvania Archives[206]

Associators

The practice of raising volunteer "Associations" for defense was based upon similar efforts taken during the French and Indian War and afterwards. Various "Associations" had been forming and weighing in on the issues facing the Province starting as early as 1774. The Philadelphia Battalions took the lead in charging forward on issues and concerns of importance. On June 10th, the "Associators of the Fourth Battalion" of the City were called upon to "meet in the usual place of parade" so that "their sense respecting a new government of the Province, and the mode proposed for obtaining it would this day be freely taken." Colonel Thomas McKeen presented the assembled Associators with several questions. All of which they answered and "carried unanimously in the Affirmative." The gathered members agreed to support the Congress and its resolves, stood willing to risk "all hazards" to support the public desires, and confirmed the "Province of Pennsylvania to be a free and independent State, and united with the other twelve Colonies." [207] The same agenda would occur, with similar results, among the remaining Associators battalions. The support of the Associators and their growing political power were recognized and courted by the proponents of a new government in the province.

The "Officers and Privates of the fifty-three Battalions of Associators of the Colony of Pennsylvania" met in Lancaster on July 4th, 1776. Those gathered conducted

---

[206] *Pennsylvania Archives*, Second Series "Pennsylvania in the War of the Revolution, Associated Battalions and Militia 1775-1783"(Afterwards *PA Archives …"War of the Revolution)* Vol 2. Ed. Egle, William H. (Harrisburg: 1888) 756. Col. Timothy Green commanding the Battalion, describes the flag as being of crimson watered silk, six feet long by five and one-half feet wide. It contained a figure garbed as a frontier rifleman, gun ready, above the motto "Liberty or Death."
[207] Ibid. 784.

elections for the two Brigadier Generals to command the Battalions and forces in the colony. Daniel Roberdeau and James Ewing were selected. The assembled representatives resolved that the commanders "shall have full power and authority to call out any number of the Associators of this Colony into action" unless superseded by higher authorities. It was further decided that "under the command and direction of our Brigadier-generals" the battalions would march to aid the "free and independent States of America."[208] The sword was drawn, the gauntlet thrown down; Pennsylvanians would again go into battle.

John Adlum of York County, fourteen years old, joined a "boys company of militia" in late 1774. His story reflects the thoughts and impressions of a young Pennsylvanian of the period. From his memoirs we read, "The newspapers had been for some time back filled with the account of the British taxing and otherwise wishing to oppress us. They began to form volunteer companies of militia in Baltimore, and the infection, if I may so call it, was brought from Baltimore to York Town..." Young Adlum continues "The boys of the town also formed a company and chose an old soldier named Dytch, who had served I one of the battalions of the Royal American Regiment" as Captain. "As we rose early and immediately went out to exercise, we became very expert in it [military drill] as well as in all our evolutions." This period of work and drill continued until July of 1776. John reflects that "There was great excitement in the country against the British ministry, and the newspapers were filled with pieces against them to keep the feelings of the people alive against taxation and other oppressions."

The Second Continental Congress voting independence. Painting by Robert Pine and Edward Savage. 148-CCD-35[209]

[208] Ibid, 1261.
[209] Pictures of the Revolutionary War. Select Audiovisual Records. National Archives and Records Administration, Washington, DC 20408. http://www.archives.gov/research/american-revolution/pictures/index.html# 021. August 24, 2005.

On July 4th 1776 the Declaration of Independence was presented in Philadelphia. In York, John wrote "We heard of the declaration of Independence on the evening of the sixth day of July." A meeting took place on the following day and the companies of the town enrolled "themselves to march to camp." John's "company of boys" departed on July 11th. "When we arrived at Philadelphia we were quartered in the barracks for a few days and then we went to Trenton by water," staying there four days. "We then marched to Elizabeth Town," and then "there was orders for us to march to Newark. In about a week we marched for Bergen and encamped within a few miles of the enemy's fleet and in full sight of them. Here it may be said that we commenced the duty of soldiers by mounting guard at various places, some near the enemy and here the Pennsylvania brigade of the Flying Camp was formed." John and many of his young friends elected to stay with new establishment and would soon find themselves engaged in the fight for independence. [210]

State Regulars

Being the most populated of the middle colonies, Pennsylvania's share of the Flying Camp was appointed to be 6,000 soldiers. Assigning Colonel Samuel Mile's Pennsylvania Riflemen and Colonel Samuel Atlee's Battalion of Musketry, both state raised units, would provide 1500 troops of the quota. Their attachment provided a solid, long term core of troops for the fight. Noted earlier as "Colonel Miles" troops, these units were specifically created to provide for the defense of the State while the Associators were dispatched elsewhere. The units were referred to as "State Regulars."

The first of these was the Pennsylvania State Rifle Regiment, also known as Colonel Samuel Miles' Regiment, it formed in March 1776. It was to consist of 1000 troops, to serve until January 1778. The regiment was armed with rifles. Organized into two battalions of six companies each, the companies numbered 78 men a piece. Samuel Miles was appointed regimental commander on March 13th. A veteran of the French and Indian War he had emerged as a Captain in 1760. He became a prosperous Philadelphia businessman, served in the state assembly, and became an active member of local patriot committees. He raised a militia company during the pre-Revolutionary disturbances, and was appointed to the Pennsylvania Committee of Safety. Colonel Miles commanded the regiment until he was captured at the Battle of Long Island on August 27th, 1776. Released during a prisoner exchange in December, he returned to Pennsylvania, and was appointed as a Brigadier General in the State forces.

The second unit was the Pennsylvania State Battalion of Musketry, known as Colonel Samuel Atlee's Battalion, was also established in March 1776. It was to be composed of "regular" troops, armed with muskets rather than rifles. The battalion was to number 500, arranged in eight companies of 58 enlisted men and three officers each. Colonel Samuel John Atlee was appointed battalion commander on March 25th. Samuel Atlee was born in Trenton, New Jersey in 1739. He served in the French and Indian War as commander of a provincial company from Lancaster County PA. He participated in the Forbes campaign and fought in the Battle of Fort Duquesne.[211] The Colonel was also

---

[210] John Adlum, *Memoirs of the Life of John Adlum in the Revolutionary War.* Ed. Howard H. Peckham. (Chicago: Caxton Club, 1968) 2-17.
[211] Jerry Kail. *Who Was Who During the American Revolution.* (New York: Bobbs-Merrill Inc.1976). 312-313.

captured in the Battle of Long Island but wasn't exchanged until August 1778. He returned to Pennsylvania but did not remain in the army. [212]

While prisoners in New York, Colonels Atlee and Miles jointly wrote to General Washington of the condition of the Americans soldiers being held there. They advised that "... respecting the American prisoners now in New York. Their situation is truly deplorable; they are now confine in the Churches in the City...." The Colonels describe a paltry diet of Salt Pork, bread, [dry ?] peas, and butter. They further noted that "they have no means of adding vegetables or any other nourishing articles for want of cash. Their being confined so long upon salt Provisions, and the common pump Water which in New York is very bad and their needing great want of Clothing, has rendered them so very unhealthy that unless something is shortly done for them they must inevitably perish." [213] The Colonel's plea for assistance for the prisoners added to the burdens and concerns General Washington carried for the Troops. Responding to his Colonels he could only inform them that "respecting the miserable State of our prisoners in New York, for want of Cloaths and Necessaries ,I have wrote to Congress on the Subject, recommending it to them, to procure a proper Credit in New York for their Supply, but I have not yet received an Answer from them." [214]

The Call to Arms

The Associations, initially, were the planned source from which 4,500 troops would be drawn. They were to raise companies from among their individual regiments which were then to be assigned to the battalions of the Pennsylvania Flying Camp. Thomas Wynne of Nantmel Township, Chester County exemplifies those who joined the Flying Camp. Born in October 1752, his family had immigrated to the New World with William Penn in 1682. On July 1st, 1776 the Revolutionary Committee of Chester County met in Downington. The fifty members present "On Motion, *Resolved*... to use their utmost endeavors ...for raising 652 men forthwith in this county..." to serve. [215] Thomas was commissioned as a Lieutenant on August 27th. He joined Colonel William Montgomery's Chester County Battalion of the Flying Camp. Lieutenant Wynne fought in the battles at Long Island and Fort Washington. He was captured and taken prisoner at the fall of the latter on November 16th. Imprisoned in the warehouses and despicable prison ships in New York, he remained a prisoner over four years, finally exchanged on January 2nd, 1781. [216]

Disadvantages existed in using the Associators to fill the quota. The most prominent being the short-term of the individual's enlistments, which made them available for service only until November 30th. [217] However, before these issues could be addressed Pennsylvania was called upon to provide immediate support to the war effort. On July 3rd, John Hancock informed the Lancaster Committee that Congress was

---

[212] Pennsylvania Historical and Museum Commission, *The Pennsylvania Line: Regimental organization and operations, 1776-1783 /by John B. B. Trussell Jr.(* hereafter noted as PA Line) (Harrisburg: The Commission, 1977). 164-167.

[213] Washington -LOC-Online. "Letter from Colonels Samuel Miles and Samuel Atlee to General Washington, November 1, 1776. 1/25/2007.

[214] Ibid. Letter from General Washington to Samuel Miles, November 25, 1776. 1/25/2007.

[215] Evelyn Abraham Benson, "Identification of Lt.Thomas Wynne of the Flying Camp, 1776" *Pennsylvania Genealogical Magazine*, Vol. 29, no.2, 1975.

[216] Ibid.

[217] Newland, 141-42.

ordering the troops for the Flying Camp to be sent to Philadelphia. They were to report "with utmost expedition" and not to await full muster but to dispatch smaller units, as they were available. [218] This directive was quickly amended by a Congressional resolution on July 4th, requiring that the available "Militia of *Pennsylvania*" go to Trenton in haste to serve until the "Flying Camp of ten thousand men" arrived. [219]

A letter from George Ross, Chairman of the Lancaster Committee relates that "the present situation of the publick [sic] affairs having made it necessary that the Militia of *Pennsylvania* should be immediately marched to the *Jerseys*, to act until the Flying Camp shall be formed … having been made known to the Associators here, they have almost to the man determined to march to this service."[220] An unknown author in Philadelphia on July 6th notes that the Philadelphia battalions were to march to Trenton and Brunswick in New Jersey. [221]

On July 14th General Washington addressed orders to the "Commanding Officer of the Pennsylvania Troops" to "proceed to Amboy, in *New Jersey, where General Mercer* is appointed to command, and there, putting yourself under his direction, receive and obey such orders as he may give."[222] Colonel Miles' Regiment marched for Amboy, arriving there on July 16th. Colonel Atlee's Battalion appeared there on July 21st. An officer's letter dated July 22nd speaks of their arrival and how "Colonel Atlee's battalion came in, and marched along the beach. They made a good appearance, and I think alarmed the enemy not a little."[223] General Hugh Mercer issued a "General Return of the Pennsylvania Forces in New Jersey" on July 25th. Listed was the regiment of Colonel Miles, first and second battalions, with the strength of 862 men. Also included was Colonel Atlee's battalion, with a recorded strength of 406 troops. The return reveals that counting "regulars" and Associators there were 3677 Pennsylvanians in New Jersey.[224]

The Pennsylvania State Regulars did not remain with the Flying Camp. General Washington ordered the two units to move to New York City in early August. Their stay in New Jersey had not been a particularly cordial affair. Colonels Atlee and Miles had refused to serve under orders of Brigadier Generals Roberdeau and Ewing. Relations between these officers were quickly strained. Both Generals had been elected to their posts as the senior officers over the Pennsylvania militia. As Colonel's Atlee and Miles had not participated in the voting they subsequently refused to serve under the Generals. [225] This account illustrates the political and personal issues existing among the "officers and gentlemen" of the period.

The Pennsylvania "State Regulars" were among the 2000 Flying Camp troops called to New York by General Washington. The Rifle Regiment and the Musketry Battalion departed Amboy on the 11th and 12th of August. The General reported in a letter of August 12th that "Colonel Miles is also here, with two battalions more of the

[218] Peter Force, Ed. *A Documentary History of the United States of America from the Declaration of Independence, July 4, 1776 to the Definitive Treaty of Peace with Great Britain, September 3, 1783,* American Archives: Fifth Series, Volumes 1/2/3, [Hereafter known as Force, *Archives,* 5th Ser, Vols. 1/,2/,3] (Washington: M. St Claire Clarke & Peter Force, 1848), Vol 1. 4.
[219] ibid. 15.
[220] ibid. 103.
[221] ibid. 34.
[222] ibid. 333.
[223] ibid. 499.
[224] Ibid. 574
[225] PA Line. 176.

Pennsylvania Riflemen." [226] Both units were assigned to Lord Stirling's Brigade. Each would see combat in the Battle of Long Island, serving with courage and valor.

General Mercer's "Return" of July 25th reflects that minus the "State Regulars" there were 2409 Pennsylvanians in service with the Flying Camp. These troops were the remaining Associators sent forth to fill the quota till the State levy could be raised. Among the units present were the first through fifth battalions of the Philadelphia Associators, Colonel Montgomery's Chester (County) battalion, and one company of the City of Philadelphia artillery. [227] Captain Benjamin Loxley was commander of the "first company of Artillery of Philadelphia." The Company had departed the City on July 21st with two twelve-pounders. It marched with a train consisting of the guns, an ammunition cart, four wagons, and fifty-nine men. The Company finally encamped at Amboy. On Tuesday, July 30th, Benjamin wrote "Now we can thourley see the Ennemy Intrenching Abrest of us, but does not attempt to fire." [228] General Mercer's return (see Figure 2) details the reported strengths of the separate units.

A General Return of the Troops in NEW-JERSEY, under the command of Brig. Gen. MERCER, July 25th, 1776.

REGIMENTS.	Colonels.	Lieut. Colonels.	Majors.	Captains.	Lieutenants.	Ensigns.	Sergeants.	Drums and fifes.	Rank and file.
Col. Miles's First Rifle Battalion	1	1	1	6	18	-	24	6	409
Col. Miles's Second Rifle Battalion	-	1	1	6	17	-	20	4	347
Pennsylvania Musketry	1	1	-	8	16	15	16	8	341
First Battalion Philadelphia Associators	1	1	1	6	12	11	24	12	360
Second Battalion Philadelphia Associators	1	1	1	7	16	14	31	15	400
Third Battalion Philadelphia Associators	1	1	2	7	12	11	26	16	310
Fourth Battalion Philadelphia Associators	1	1	1	6	16	8	28	11	285
Fifth Battalion Philadelphia Associators	-	1	1	4	13	-	17	6	180
Colonel Montgomery, Chester	1	1	1	6	15	8	27	11	290
Artillery from New-Jersey, six pieces	-	-	-	-	-	-	-	-	120
Artillery from Philadelphia, two pieces	-	-	-	-	-	-	-	-	50
Total	7	9	9	56	135	67	213	89	3,092

Brigadier-General *Roberdeau.*

STATIONED.

At *Newark* Ferry, rank and file	122
Artillery at *Newark* Ferry, 2 pieces, Matrosses	20
At *Elizabeth-Town* and its posts, rank and file	500
Artillery at *Elizabeth-Town,* two pieces, Matrosses	20
At *Woodbridge* and its posts, rank and file	577
Artillery at *Woodbridge,* two pieces, Matrosses	20
At *Amboy* and its posts, rank and file	1,723
Artillery at *Amboy,* four pieces, Matrosses	110
	3,092

Figure 2. Force, *Archives,* 5th Ser, Vol. 1. 574.

Another return was issued on August 14th which provided an accounting of his forces in New Jersey. It reflects the dispatch of 2075 troops to New York. Among the

---

[226] Force, *Archives,* 5th Ser, Vol. 1. 910.
[227] ibid. 574.
[228] Benjamin Loxley. *A Journal of the Campaign to Amboy of the Parts of Jersey, 1776.* Historical Society of Pennsylvania, Philadelphia, PA.

remaining troops the five Philadelphia battalions accounted for 1169 rank and file "Present fit for duty" [229] (see Figure 3).

A General Return of the Army in New-Jersey, under the Command of the Honourable Hugh Mercer, Brigadier-General in the Continental service; Perth-Amboy, August 14, 1776.

	Commissioned Officers present.							Staff Officers.					Non-Com'd Officers.		Rank and File.			
	Colonels.	Lieut. Colonels.	Majors.	Captains.	1st Lieutenants.	2d Lieutenants.	Ensigns.	Chaplains.	Adjutants.	Quartermasters.	Surgeons.	Mates.	Sergeants.	Drums and Fifes.	Present fit for duty.	Sick.	On furlough.	Total.
Colonel Thompson	1	1	1	8	7	-	7	-	1	1	-	-	28	15	386	14	2	402
Colonel Reed............................	1	1	1	5	5	-	5	-	1	1	-	-	18	6	252	8	-	266
Colonel Dickinson.......................	1	1	2	8	7	7	11	-	1	1	1	2	25	12	263	8	24	299
Second Battalion, Colonel Buyard.........	1	1	2	8	8	8	8	1	1	1	1	1	31	10	309	-	-	309
Third Battalion, Colonel Cadwalader.......	1	1	2	7	7	8	11	-	1	1	1	1	33	14	339	7	13	357
Fourth Battalion, Colonel McKean.........	1	1	2	5	6	7	9	-	1	1	1	1	28	12	162	11	-	173
Fifth Battalion, Colonel Clymer...........	-	1	2	3	8	5	-	-	1	1	1	1	14	6	96	13	6	115
Major McVain............................	-	-	1	4	4	4	5	-	1	-	1	-	17	9	138	-	-	138
Colonel Montgomery......................	1	-	1	8	9	8	8	1	1	1	1	1	28	7	388	5	1	193
First Battalion of Cumberland.............	-	-	-	2	2	2	2	-	-	-	-	-	8	4	121	1	-	122
Colonel Hill.............................	-	-	2	3	7	-	2	-	-	1	-	-	10	6	153	1	-	154
Colonel Dill, Fifth Battalion York County....	-	-	1	2	3	2	2	-	-	-	-	-	6	-	63	-	-	63
Colonel Guyger..........................	-	-	-	3	3	3	2	-	-	-	-	-	12	6	104	-	-	104
Colonel Hart............................	-	-	-	1	1	1	1	-	-	-	-	-	4	2	58	-	-	58
Colonel Lewis...........................	-	-	1	1	1	2	-	1	-	-	-	-	4	-	46	-	-	46
Colonel Moore..........................	1	1	2	5	6	6	4	1	1	1	1	-	20	6	191	10	2	203
Colonel Ross............................	-	-	1	2	5	-	3	-	-	-	-	-	14	5	124	-	-	124
Lieutenant-Colonel Donaldson.............	-	1	1	6	6	5	6	-	1	1	1	-	23	8	254	2	2	258
Colonel Grub...........................	1	1	1	11	11	11	11	-	-	-	-	-	44	19	335	-	6	341
Colonel Thomas.........................	1	1	1	3	3	3	3	-	1	1	1	-	24	6	150	-	-	150
																		4,070
Troops sent to New-York..................	2	4	5	37	48	37	25	2	4	4	3	3	123	59	2,075			

To His Excellency General *Washington*, Head-Quarters, *New-York.*

Figure 3. Force, *Archives*, 5th Ser, Vol. 1. 964.

Several of the Association battalions and Pennsylvania Flying Camp units would serve in the New York campaigns of 1776. Among these was the Second Battalion of Philadelphia Associators which appears to have been ordered to New York in mid-August. [230] The Third Battalion of the Philadelphia Associators was transferred to New York around August 19th. [231] Among others from the State was a Colonel Samuel Burd who was commanding a battalion of the Lancaster County Associators. On August 12th he was ordered to march "with about three hundred men of the Flying Camp, including one company of riflemen, volunteers from Cumberland, commanded by Captain Steel."[232] Cumberland County had organized twelve companies which marched forth to the Flying Camp by August 17th. Four more companies were being prepared to follow. [233]

Lieutenant Colonel Peter Kiechlein (Keichlein) commanded a battalion of Associators from Northampton County, specifically raised in July for the Pennsylvania (PA) Flying Camp. The battalion was assigned to Lord Stirling's Brigade and participated in the Battle of Long Island. Also listed among the participating units in the battle was a Berks County (PA) Flying Camp battalion commanded by Lieutenant Colonel Nicholas

---

[229] Force, *Archives*, 5th Ser, Vol. 1. 963.
[230] ibid. 909.
[231] ibid. 983.
[232] ibid. 909.
[233] ibid.994-995

Lutz, and the 1st Pennsylvania (PA) Flying Camp under Colonel James Cunningham, and the 2nd PA Flying Camp led by Colonel Henry Haller. [234]

Michael Graham (1758-1834) was a member of Captain I. Collier's Lancaster County Company assigned to the Pennsylvania Flying Camp. His account of the battle, submitted as a pension application in 1832, reflects the confusion and terror of an eighteen year old in combat.

> About the last of May or first of June, 1776...I turned out a volunteer in a company... We composed a part of the corps denominated the Flying Camp." The company's journey eventually ended in New York. "We were taken to Long Island and stationed at Brooklyn... The day before the battle, eight men were taken from the company to which I belonged on picket guard ...I was one of that number." The guard was posted on a road near Flatbush. "We continued at our post until I think about twelve o'clock when an officer came and told us to make our escape, for we were surrounded. We immediately retreated towards our camp. We had went but a small distance before we saw the enemy ... before us. We ... posted ourselves behind a stone fence; from the movements of the enemy, we had soon to move from this position. Here we got parted, and I neither saw officers or men belonging to our party during the balance of that day. I had went but a small distance before I came to a party of our men making a bold stand. I stopped and took one fire at the enemy, but they came on with such rapidity that I retreated back into the woods. [The firing having ended from the point young Graham had retreated from he returned to the place.]

> I had not been at this place I think more than one minute before the British came in a different direction from where they were when I retreated, firing platoons as they marched. I turned and took one fire at them and then made my escape as fast as I could. By this time our troops were routed in every direction. It is impossible for me to describe the confusion and horror of the scene that ensued: the artillery flying with the chains over the horses' backs, our men running in almost every direction, and run which way they would, they were almost sure to meet the British or Hessians... I escaped by getting behind the British that had been engaged with Lord Stirling and entered a swamp or marsh through which a great many of our men were retreating. Some of them were mired and crying to their fellows for God's sake to help them out; but every man was intent on his own safety and no assistance was rendered. Soon after I entered the marsh, a cannonading commenced from our batteries on the British, and they retreated, and I got safely into camp. Out of the eight men that were taken from the company to which I belonged the day before the battle on guard, I only escaped. The others were either killed or taken prisoners. [235]

A Difficult Path to March

---

[234] Eric I Meadows. *The Battle of Long Island.*(Monmouth Beach NJ: Frenew Press, 1978). Appendix B, D.
[235] .Michael Graham. *The Revolution Remembered : Eyewitness Accounts of the War for Independence.* Edited by John C. Dann. (Chicago: University of Chicago Press, 1980).48-50.

What may appear as a quick and substantial response to filling the Flying Camp quota overshadows the true difficulties of raising the planned ten thousand men. A report from General Mercer on August 4th notes that "only 274 rank and file properly belonging to the Flying Camp" were counted among the troops in New Jersey. These numbers show improvement in an October 8th report reflecting 2,615 Pennsylvania Flying Camp members. [236] Major problems delayed the raising of the forces. One was the decision of Congress to increase the quotas for the Flying Camp. Another was the desertion of troops, especially those from Pennsylvania.

The first difficulty presented itself when on July 22nd John Hancock wrote the Pennsylvania Convention, "As it is impossible to ascertain the strength of our enimie, or the force destined for the attack of *New York,* it is incumbent on us to be prepared... For this purpose, the Congress have come to a resolution to increase the Flying Camp. I have it therefore in command from Congress to request, that you will immediately augment your quota for the Flying Camp with four battalions of militia, in addition to those formerly desired by Congress." [237] The Pennsylvania Convention accepted the requested increase in the quota. On August 7th it established a committee "to consider of the most effectual and expeditious measures for raising the quota of this state for the Flying Camp. "[238] On August 10th it considered the committee "draft of an Ordnance" that formed the basis for establishing the Pennsylvania Flying Camp; a copy follows:

Saturday, August 10, 1776, A.M

The Convention met pursuant to adjournment.
According to the Order of the Day, the draft of the Ordnance respecting the Flying Camp was read by paragraphs, and after long debates thereon, the House came to the following Resolutions:
1st. Resolved, That the Commanding Officers of the several Battalions in the respective Counties of this State, immediately march in *Jersey,* with their whole Battalions.
2d. Resolved, That the Associators of the Counties *of Bedford, Northumberland, Northampton,* and *Westmoreland,* and the Guards of the City of *Philadelphia,* retained by the Council of Safety, and the two Companies of Colonel *Ross's* Battalion, and the two Companies of Colonel *Slough's* Battalion, of about fifty men each, left to guard the prisoners, and about sixty carpenters and workmen, retained by the Committee of *Lancaster,* be excepted out of the foregoing resolve.
3d. Resolved, That a Bounty of three pounds be paid to every Associator who has entered or will enter into the service in the Flying Camp, to continue until the first day of *January* next, if not sooner discharged, excepting such as have already received a Bounty.
4th. Resolved, *That* such Battalions as have or shall furnish their quotas for the Flying Camp, and have been in actual service six weeks, shall be permitted to return home, if the Generals and Field-Officers shall judge it consistent with the publick safety; and when the whole cannot be

[236] William H Eggle, Ed. *Pennsylvania in the War of the Revolution, Associated Battalions and Militia 1775-1783,* Vol.2 (Harrisburg: E. K. Meyers, 1888), 761.
[237] Force, *Archives,* 5th Ser, Vol. 1. 495.
[238] Force, *Archives,* 5th Ser, Vol. 2. 18.

permitted to return, furloughs are to be granted in cases of particular necessity.

5th. *Resolved,* That three Commissioners be appointed to go to Head-Quarters in *Jersey,* to form the Flying Camp.

6th .*Resolved,* That the Commissioners , with the field Officers of the Counties respectfully, shall nominate the Officers of the Flying Camp, where they are not already nominated.

7th. *Resolved ,* That Money be put into the hands of the Commissioners for the purpose of paying the Bounty. [239]

A second committee was founded to consider the request for raising the additional quota of four battalions. On August 12th the Convention met, considered the committee report, and resolved to "fix the quota of the four additional Battalions for the Flying–Camp" (see Table 5).

City of Philadelphia	628
County of Philadelphia	160
" " Bucks	100
" " Chester	160
" " Lancaster	323
" " Berks	240
" " York	515
" " Northampton	278
" " Cumberland	580

Table 5. Force, *Archives,* 5th Ser, Vol. 2. 20.

Progress was made in raising the dedicated Pennsylvania Flying Camp battalions to replace the temporarily assigned Associators. The additional complication of high desertion rates still severely strained the efforts to provide the forces needed. Benjamin Loxley provides in his journal evidence of early dissatisfactions and discontent among some of the Associators. He records a General Order, dated August 1st.

The General is very sorry that he is under the necessity of reminding some of the Pennsylvania Associators of the terms on which they Agreed to Serve here, namely to remain on duty untill a suffient number of troops had joined to form the flying camp and while on duty to conform to the Regulations of the Continental Army. Such of the NonCommissioned officers or soldiers as shall Discover a contrary disposition will subject themselves to punishment. If any shall presume to quit their post under pretense of their time limmitted for serving being expired they will be treated in every respect as deserters from the Continental Army. [240]

---

[239] Ibid. 19-20.
[240] Loxley, August 1st 1776.

On August 4th General Mercer wrote to John Hancock,"…some of the Militia from *Pennsylvania,* not duly informed of the length of time their services here might be required have become much dissatisfied. It is with difficulty the officers in some of the battalions prevent a desertion, not of men singly, but by companies." [241]   The situation appeared sufficiently serious to warrant informing General Washington. On August 8th, General Washington wrote an open letter to the Pennsylvania Associators. He refers to an "impatience to return home" and "less honorable motives" regarding continued service by the troops. The letter serves as an example of the difficulties he faced in fielding a viable army:

Head-Quarters, August 8, 1776

GENTLEMEN: I had fully resolved to pay you a visit in *New-Jersey,* if the movements of the enemy, and some late intelligence, indicating an early attack, had not induced me to suspend it. Allow me, therefore, to address you in this mode, as fellow-citizens and fellow-soldiers engaged in the same glorious cause; to represent to you that the fate of your country depends, in all human probability, on the exertion of a few weeks; that it is of the utmost importance to keep up a respectable force for that time; and there can be no doubt that success will crown our efforts, if we firmly and resolutely determine to conquer or die. I have placed so much confidence in the spirit and zeal of the Associated Troops of *Pennsylvania,* that I cannot persuade myself an impatience to return home, or a less honorable motive, will defeat my well-grounded expectation that they will do their country essential service at this critical time, when the powers of despotism are all combined against it, and ready to strike their most decisive stroke. If I could allow myself to doubt your spirit and perseverance, I should represent the ruinous consequences of your leaving the service, by setting before you the discouragement it would give to the Army, the confusion and shame of our friends, and the still more galling triumph of our enemies; but as I have no such doubts, I shall only thank you for the spirit and ardour you have shown in so readily marching to meet the enemy, and am most confident you will crown it by glorious perserverance. The honor and safety of our bleeding country, and every other motive that can influence the brave and heroick patriot, call loudly upon us to acquit ourselves with spirit. In short, we must now determine to be enslaved or free. If we make freedom our choice, we must obtain it by the blessing of Heaven on our united and vigorous efforts.

I salute you, gentlemen, most affectionently, and beg leave to remind you that liberty, honour, and safety, are all at stake; and I trust Providence will smile upon our efforts, and establish us once more the inhabitians of a free and happy country.

I am, gentlemen, you most humble servant,

Go. Washington [242]

Responding to his Commander-in-Chief's letter on August 9th Mercer writes, "A cowardly infamous spirit of desertion prevails here too much. Your letter will be read to

---

[241] Force, *Archives,* 5th Ser, Vol. 1. 750.
[242] Ibid. 849-851

each corps, and must have good effects."[243]   On August 11th, he again took up pen and quill to write, "The *Pennsylvania* Associators continue to desert by bodies. Seventeen went off from the fourth battalion last night, and am just now informed of another party, who have left camp. I hear several companies about to join, and hope still to keep up a formidable appearance."[244]   He attempted to quell the increasing flow of desertions. On August 10th he wrote to General Dickinson of Pennsylvania, commanding troops in the Elizabethtown area. He relates writing to the "Convention of *New Jersey,* acquainting them of the desertion of numbers of the *Pennsylvania* militia, and desiring them to order out the militia to guard the ferries and other effectual steps to secure the deserters." He noted having written to Congress and advising them "of the unhappy condition of the Militia" and the impact that the losses through desertions were having on his command.[245]   A letter from an unknown officer to General Dickinson provides "the [blank] company seem determined to go off tomorrow morning. Their going will, in my opinion, be followed by the First battalion and the rest. The present is a matter of infinite consequence if Colonel Dickinson will give his sentiments to the battalion this afternoon, I am convinced it would be effectual in quieting the present disturbance."[246]

    August 11th, Mercer's General Order of the day addressed the Pennsylvania and New Jersey troops "…they have it now in the power to render the most essential service to their country by Reinforcing the Army at New York his Excellency George Washington will consider any assistance he may receive at this time the greatest obligation such Troops as turn out voluntarily on that Service will have their names enroll among the bravest of the Americans." He followed this with instructions for a return to be made by each battalion, listing deserters. [247]   Writing to John Hancock on August 12th General Mercer comments that "Notwithstanding the desertion of many of the Associators, we shall have a respectable force here. The militia of this state [New Jersey] are to be arranged universally: the greatest number by far of the P*ennsylvania* gentlemen are activated by the most laudable spirit, and voluntarily engage to serve their country wherever they are required to go."[248]   How the New Jersey militia filled the void created by the desertions is reflected in a letter from William Livingston to General Washington, August 12th.

    William Livingston was the Brigadier General in command of the New Jersey Militia. He eventually became the first Governor of the State. In his letter he notes that "a considerable body of the militia must be kept here to supply the place of the Pennsylvania Associators, who are deserting their post in considerable numbers, not withstanding the most spirited exertions of their officers, and particularly their colonel [Dickinson?], whose behavior does honor his province, in particular and America in general. We have taken such measures as I hope will put a stop to any further behavior of this kind." General Livingston further comments that no work to improve the defenses and fortifications had been accomplished in the area since the Pennsylvania units had relieved his militia. He related that as soon as the militia had replaced the Pennsylvanians he would ensure the work was "prosecuted with all possible vigor" to improve the defenses.[249]

---

[243] Ibid.894.
[244] Ibid.
[245] Ibid. 895.
[246] Ibid. The name /designator of the Company is redacted from the original source.
[247] Loxley, August 11th, 1776

[248] Force, *Archives,* 5th Ser, Vol. 1.908.
[249] Ibid.910

The desertion of Pennsylvania troops concerned the highest levels of the State government. The Council of Safety, on August 11th, ordered "That all commanding officers of each Battalion or company of Associators... be required to .. [provide] a list of the names of [those] who have deserted."[250]   The Pennsylvania Convention considered the issue of desertion on August 16th beginning with a reading of a letter from Colonel Dickinson. The Colonel complained of desertions by the Associators and implored the Convention to provide a remedy to the problem. The Convention resolved that all deserters would be granted an amnesty of eight days to return to their units without recrimination. Those failing to return were to be arrested and tried for desertion. Those leaving without authority after that were to receive no clemency and would face trial. Commanders marching their units to New Jersey were to apprehend all deserters they encountered and return them to the Camp. Finally, the Convention expressed that "the Associators are therefore assured, that as soon as the Flying Camp is formed, and the publick safety will admit, they shall be permitted to return home." [251]

Positive results were achieved through the combined efforts of military and civilian leaders to establish the Pennsylvania Flying Camp and deal with desertions. By early September some of the first assigned Associators battalions were being relieved from service. The orderly book of the Chester County Associators illustrates the results of these efforts. On September 1st the record states " Coll [colonel] Barton's Batt [battalion] of Pennsylvania Infantry of North Hemton county Have furnished their quota of the flying camp and served six weeks being from their local cituation exposed it to frequent attacks of the Indians have permission to return home." The Orderly Book continues with details from entries dated September 6th. Battalions from Pennsylvania who hadn't supplied their quota for the Flying Camp were ordered to do so by that afternoon. They were advised that the State Convention had ordered not to allow any of them to return until they had served the required six weeks in camp and "furnished their quota." In the September 8th entries is found "Coll Lewis' Batt of the Pennsylvania Associators having Done their Duty as good and orderly soldiers and furnished a complete company for the flying camp are Dismised..."[252] On September 9th "The officers and soldiers of Colonel Hart's battalion of Pennsylvania Associators having done their duty as good and orderly soldiers, and having furnished a company for the Flying Camp, are hereby discharged the service of the *States,* and permitted to return home."[253] Also recorded are the dismissals of Captains Sheet's and Potts companies of Colonel Hill's Battalion . On September 10th an entry appears in the Chester County Battalion Orderly Book reflecting the release of Colonel Butt's Battalion.[254] Many individual Associators volunteered to remain in service after their units were discharged. In October, at White Plains, over 100 men from Pennsylvania enlisted in the newly formed Continental battalion. General Washington was advised that "many of the *Pennsylvanians* in the Flying Camp are willing to enter into the service on the new establishment." [255]

In November, regiments of the Pennsylvania Flying Camp were posted at Fort Lee along the Hudson River. There they were under the command of General Nathanael Greene. When General Howe's forces threatened Fort Washington on the opposite shore

[250] Ibid.962
[251] Force, *Archives*, 5[h] Ser, Vol. 2. 22.
[252] William Armstrong, *Orderly Book 1776,178-1779*. Historical Society of Pennsylvania, Philadelphia, PA.
[253] Force, *Archives*, 5[h] Ser, Vol. 2. 256.
[254] Armstrong.September 10, 1776.
[255] Force, *Archives*, 5[h] Ser, Vol. 2. 1202.

General Greene elected to reinforce the garrison. In a November 3rd letter to Colonel Robert Magaw, commanding the fort, General Greene informed "I am directed by his Excellency General Washington to remove Col Hutchinsons Regiment over to this post and to send you another.... I shall send you Col Backsters (Baxter's) Regiment...." [256] Colonel William Baxter's Bucks County Regiment was subsequently sent across the river to boaster Fort Washington's defenses. This would prove to be an unfortunate assignment for Colonel Baxter. He was killed in action at the battle for the fort on November 16th. [257] His regiment, along with the full garrison of Fort Washington was forced to surrender. Approximately 2900 soldiers were taken prisoner. [258]

The final weeks of December 1776 witnessed the Pennsylvanian's retreat with the American army across New Jersey. Most of the battalions had completed their terms of enlistment. Others remained with the Army, fighting in the battles of Trenton and Princeton. It was during this low period for the American cause that the headstrong Pennsylvania Associators would act independently once more, influencing the outcome of war.

Colonel Cadwalader[259]

John Cadwalader was a native Philadelphian. He originally captained the "Silk Stocking Company" which was composed of young men from the high society of the City. Cadwalader was considered a gentleman of polished manners and a bold, brave soldier. Twice he declined promotions to the rank of Brigadier General in the Continental Army. General Washington spoke of him as "a man of ability, a good disciplinarian, firm in his principles, and of intrepid bravery." [260] He had been taken prisoner at the fall of Fort Washington. Because he had "showed some civilities to General *Prescott* when prisoner; of this the General made mention to Sir *William Howe*, who was pleased to order his immediate release, without parole, or even injunction not to serve the Congress."[261]

[256] Nathanael Greene. *The Papers of Nathanael Greene*, (Chapel Hill NC: University of North Carolina Press, 1976), Vol. 1. 331.
[257] Force, *Archives*, 5th Ser, Vol.3. 729.
[258] Nathanael Greene. Vol. 1. 358n.
[259] William S Stryker. *The Battles of Trenton and Princeton*. (Boston: Houghton, Mifflin and Co, The Riverside Press, 1898), 81.
[260] Ibid. 81.
[261] Force, *Archives*, 5h Ser, Vol. 3. 840.

Colonel Cadwalader went on to distinguished service in the Battles of Princeton, and later Germantown and Monmouth.

In early July Colonel Cadwalader was leading the Third Philadelphia Battalion, assigned under the command of General Mercer. He and his unit had served in the Flying Camp as part of the State's initial commitment. In December he was commanding a Brigade and was part of General Washington's plan for the assault against Trenton.[262] The Brigade consisted of 1200 men from four Philadelphia Militia units, a Delaware Militia company, and two Philadelphia artillery companies.[263] On December 12th orders were issued for Cadwalader's force of 1200 soldiers, to be stationed south of Trenton. He was instructed to "post your brigade at and near *Bristol*," and there to "establish the necessary guards and throw up some little redoubts at *Dunk's Ferry* and the different passes in *Neshamini.*" General Washington called upon the Colonel to "spare no pains or expense to get intelligence of the enemy's motions and intentions." His orders in the event of an enemy assault were "in a word, you are to give them all the opposition you can, without hazarding the loss of your brigade." [264] On December 21st Cadwalader's force was augmented by Colonel Daniel Hitchcock's Brigade of about 600 New England Continentals.[265]

The Colonel's increased force, of about 1800 men, was in place to return to New Jersey. The plan set in motion on December 25th detailed his force to cross at Neshaminy Ferry and land at Burlington "with view to a direct attack upon" Colonel von Donop's Hessian Grenadiers and Colonel Stirling's Highlanders stationed in Bordertown. [266] Hopefully quashing the latter's potential to advance to the assistance of Colonel Rall at Trenton. All plans though are susceptible to the vagaries of nature and on December 26th Colonel Cadwalader wrote to General Washington "Sir: The river was so full of ice that it was impossible to pass above *Bristol*, where I intended, and therefore concluded to make an attempt at *Dunk's Ferry.*" He explained he was unable to move artillery across the river to support those who had reached the other side. He wrote that "Upon reporting this to the field-officers, they were all of opinion that it would not be proper to proceed without cannon." It was jointly concluded by this field committee to withdraw from New Jersey. The soldiers returning to the Pennsylvania shore did so "with great reluctance" as reported by Colonel Joseph Reed. [267]

Unaware of Washington's earlier crossing, John Cadwalader made a second, and this time, successful attempt on December 27th to take his force across the Delaware. Writing that day to General Washington he provided;

> Sir; As I did not hear from you this morning, and being prepared to embark, I concluded you were still on this side, and therefore embarked and landed about fifteen hundred men, about two miles above *Bristol* . After a considerable number were landed, I had information... that you had crossed over from *Trenton*. This defeated the scheme of joining your Army. We were much embarrassed which way to proceed. I thought it most prudent to retreat, but Colonel *Reed* was of opinion that

---

[262] Cadwalader was promoted to Brigadier General of Pennsylvania Militia in late December.
[263] Samuel Stelle Smith. *The Battle of Trenton.* (Monouth Beach, NJ: Philip Freneau Press, 1965), 28.
[264] Force, *Archives*, 5ʰ Ser, Vol. 3. 1185.
[265] Stryker. 59.
[266] Henry B Carrington.*Battles of the American Revolution 1775-1781.* (New York: A S Barnes, 1876), 271.
[267] David Hackett Fischer. *Washington's Crossing.* (New York: Oxford University Press, 2004). 215.

we might safely proceed to *Burlington,* and recommended it warmly, least it should have a bad effect on the Militia, who were twice disappointed.

Colonel Cadwalader reported the departure of the enemy forces from the area, to include Bordertown. He added that;

This information has induced me to proceed, though not quite conformable to your orders which I received on the march this afternoon. If you should think proper to cross over, a pursuit would keep up the panick. They went off with great precipitation, and pressed all the wagons in their reach." The newly emboldened Colonel finished his report with "I shall write you to-morrow, I hope from *Trenton."* [268]

Colonel Reed's warm recommendations seem an encouragement to the initially reluctant Cadwalader to act and seize the initiative. General Washington, always ready to act upon such an opportunity, made a similar decision. The Pennsylvanians, and especially Colonel Reed, had taken whip in hand and driven the assault forward. At Washington's Headquarters a council of war was held in the late evening of December 27th. An initial reluctance to expand upon the victory at Trenton evolved into the idea that "a bold stroke could liberate a large part of New Jersey" and "demonstrate that the success at Trenton was not an accident."[269]

A letter to Colonel Cadwalader from Washington's aide de camp Colonel Tench Tilghman, written at "ten at night" that evening, set the stage for the second of Washington's crossings. Tilghman wrote "Dear Sir: I am commanded by his Excellency to inform you that since he wrote you this morning... he has heard that you have passed over this day. ... The General will cross the day after to-morrow with the Continental battalion. ... He therefore desires that you would keep your ground, and not attempt anything,(without you see a certainty of success) till he passes the river. ...I think it will be very hard if we cannot, by a junction of our forces, put Count *Donnop* to the rout." [270] The dogged determination of the Pennsylvania Associators, Colonel Reed, and Colonel Cadwalader combined to place in motion the subsequent American victory at Princeton.

In addition to Cadwalader's forces, General James Ewing and his brigade, consisting mostly of the remains of the Pennsylvania Flying Camp and some New Jersey militia troops, also crossed over the river. Ewing, a native Pennsylvanian, of Scot-Irish decent, came from the then western frontier region of Lancaster County. He had been a Lieutenant in the militia during the French and Indian War. He served in the Assembly from 1771 to 1775.[271] As previously noted, he was commissioned a Brigadier General in July 1776. In December, Ewing's Brigade consisted of two Cumberland County regiments, and a regiment each from Lancaster, York, and Chester Counties.[272] The "small body" of New Jersey militia assigned was commanded by Brigadier General

[268] Force, *Archives,* 5[h] Ser, Vol. 3. 1147.

[269] Fischer. 266.

[270] Force, *Archives,* 5[h] Ser, Vol. 3.1447-48.

[271] Purcell. *Who Was Who in the American Revolution.* 156.

[272] Force, *Archives,* 5[h] Ser, Vol. 3. 1401, The *Return of Forces...* dated December 22nd 1776 reflects the units noted. Smith in his *The Battle of Trenton* adds a Bucks County militia regiment under Colonel Joseph Hart. General Washington's orders to Ewing, dated December 12th, include the assignment of "A part of Colonel *Hart's* battlion" to Ewing.

Philemon Dickinson and was posted at Yardley's Ferry and along the adjacent river bank.[273]

Earlier in December Ewing's command was ordered to "guard the river *Delaware*, from the ferry opposite (Trenton) to *Border*-Town, till you come within two miles of thereabouts of *Yardley's* Mill, to which General *Dickinson's* command will extend." Ewing was encouragingly told that "so much depends upon your watchfulness, that you cannot possibly be too much upon your guard." Instructions included the posting of guards and sentries along his line. It was stressed that good intelligence was essential to the successful outcome of the operations. He was directed "to spare no pains nor cost to gain information of the enemy's movements or designs. Whatever sums you pay to obtain this end, I will cheerfully refund. Every piece of information worthy of communication transmit to me without loss of time." [274]

Once he was in position along the Delaware River Ewing took the liberty to bloody the enemy garrison in Trenton. He orchestrated several raids upon the Hessian's occupying the town and adjacent ferry crossings. His efforts helped to disrupt Colonel Rall's command and prevent the Germans from establishing quiet and easy winter quarters. Instead they were forced into maintaining a constant state of readiness. Concurrent New Jersey militia raids upon adjacent positions increased the pressure upon the Germans.

In the planned assault upon Trenton, General Ewing's brigade was to cross the Delaware at the Trenton Ferry. His force was to secure the bridge over the Assunpink Creek, denying a southern escape route from the town. The day of the attack found Ewing's command being battered by the severe winter storm enveloping the region. Delayed in crossing, the Pennsylvanians found their advanced blocked by massive ice jams. In a December 27th letter to John Hancock, General Washington states;

> General *Ewing* was to have crossed before day at *Trenton Ferry*, and
> taken possession of the bridge leading out of town; but the quantity of ice
> was so great, that though he did everything in his power to effect it, he
> could not get over. ... I am fully confident that could the troops under
> Generals *Ewing* and *Cadwalader* have passed the river, I should have
> been able, with their assistance, to have driven the enemy from all their
> posts below *Trenton*. [275]

On December 30th, General Washington again crossed over the Delaware River, this time at McKonkley's Ferry. The rest of his army crossed over during the day, including those at Trenton Ferry. Many of the men in Ewing's Brigade were due release from their service on January 1st. As early as November 30th General Washington had expressed concerns over their remaining with the Army. In a letter to John Hancock he wrote, "I have no assurances that more than a very few of the troops composing the Flying Camp will remain after the time of their engagement is out; so far from it, I am told that some of General *Ewing's* brigade, who stand engaged to the 1st of January, are now going away." [276] The General's concerns would rise to face him at one of the most critical times during the entire campaign.

---

[273] Stryker. 82-83.
[274] Force, *Archives*, 5[h] Ser, Vol. 3. 1184.
[275] Ibid, 1444.
[276] Ibid, 919.

A large number of the "old soldiers" of the Army were due to complete their terms of service on the last day of the year. In his post-war memoir a "sergeant" writes about the condition of the troops after the Battle of Trenton. It was "at this time our troops were in a destitute condition. The horses attached to our cannon were without shoes…over the ice they would slide in every direction. Our men…were without shoes…comfortable clothing and …as traces of our march towards Princeton, the ground was … marked with the blood of the soldiers feet." [277] The Pennsylvania Flying Camp troops would have suffered the same depravations. A serious effort was put forth by the Washington's general officers, and by himself, to convince the troops of the Flying Camp to remain with his forces at the critical moment. General Henry Knox spoke to the soldiers on December 31st, urging them to remain a "few days longer." General Thomas Mifflin of Pennsylvania rode up to Trenton from Bordertown to address the men. He is reported to have "urged them with the most patriotic appeals to stand by the cause of independence." The effort had some success as reportedly 1400 of the troops were to "poise their firelocks as a sign that they consented" to remain.[278] General Washington comments in a January 1st, 1777 letter to John Hancock, "After much persuasion and the exertions of their Officers, half or a greater proportion of those from the Eastward have consented to stay Six Weeks, on a bounty of Ten dollars. I feel the inconvenience of this advance and I know the consequences which will result from it; But what could be done? Pennsylvania had allowed the same to her Militia." [279] It appears that the men of the Pennsylvania Flying Camp did not elect to remain in large number. After January 1st, little record of the regiments in General Ewing's brigade appears. General Ewing does not appear among the forces at Trenton and Princeton. It appears that many of the Pennsylvania Flying Camp members withheld from the call to "poise their firelocks."

The Flying Camp's service has been called "inglorious." [280] Pennsylvania strove to raise its quota while beleaguered by confusion, opposition, discontent, and desertion. Those soldiers who stepped forth experienced the mayhem of battle and the tedium of garrison duty. Yet their dogged determination provided strong service to the Nation at a time of weakness; hardly an "inglorious" existence.

[277] William S. Stryker. "The Princeton Surprise 1777" reprinted from the *Magazine of American History, August 1882*. Pamphete published by A.S. Barnes & Co, New York. *Pamphlets in American History*, Group 1, (microform).(Sanford, NC:Microfilming Corporation of America,1979). No. RW 311.
[278] Stryker. *The Battles of Trenton and Princeton*. 254-256.
[279] Washington - LOC Online, Letter to Continental Congress "Trenton, January 1, 1777" (12/21/05).
[280] Francis E Devine. "The Pennsylvania Flying Camp, July-November 1776". *Pennsylvania History*. (January 1979) Vol.4 pp 59-78.

Chapter 6
New Jersey

"Cockpit of the Revolution."[281]

In November 1775, the atmosphere among the people of the "marshes and peaceful farms" of New Jersey was described as " Battalions of Militia & Minute-Men embodying- Drums & Fifes rattling- Military Language in every Mouth-Numbers who a few Days ago were plain Countrymen have now clothed themselves in martial Forms- Powered Hair sharp pinched Beavers-Uniform in Dress with their Battalion- Swords on their Thighs- & stern in the Art of War- Resolved, in steady manly Firmness, to support & establish American Liberty, or die in Battle."[282] This idyllic view is tempered by the reality that only a portion of the people actually supported the revolution. A large part of the citizenry remained loyal to the Crown. Many more remained aloof, wishing not to be involved with either side of the conflict. The State would become a hotbed of revolt and a battlefield to be repeatedly fought over.

Early in 1776 the New Jersey Militia had been called upon to aid in the defense of New York City. Much of the militia had left the State to serve under General Washington in New York. Hardly had they arrived there though than a clamoring to return home ensued. The inhabitants of New Jersey were alarmed by the threat represented by the British forces. The departure of their militia left the people feeling unprotected against the threats. Word of such concerns naturally reached the militia men stationed around New York. [283]

Their fears were increased by British raids, the presence of the enemy fleet in local waters, and the rising conflict with Loyalist in the State. Concerns over the threat to New Jersey were not confined to the local leadership and citizenry. In Philadelphia on July 5th "Measures for the Defence of New-Jersey and Pennsylvania" were discussed "At a Conference of the Delegates in Congress for the States of *New-York, New-Jersey,* and *Pennsylvania,* of the Committee of Safety of *Pennsylvania*, the Committee of Inspection and Observation for the City and Liberties of *Philadelphia,* and the Field-Officers of the five Battalions of the said city, which" occurred at the State House. The conferees were tasked to determine "the best means of defending the Colonies of *New-Jersey* and *Pennsylvania."* From this conference several actions that we've already noted were decided upon. Among these was the dispatch of "all the associated Militia of *Pennsylvania,"* to serve temporarily in the Flying Camp; the marching of the three (PA) State Regulars battalions to New Jersey; and the movement of Colonel Hazlet's Delaware troops to positions in the state. [284]

On July 5th General Washington wrote to Brigadier General William Livingston, "The situation of *New-Jersey* is such; and the apprehensions of the inhabitants so justly excited, that I have concluded to discharge the militia from this place, except those from Morris county... The remainder of the militia I have dismissed... but have not discharged them as I am of opinion apart of them maybe usefully employed in the immediate defence of the Province. In this view they fall properly under your command..." [285] General

---

[281] Leonard Lundin. *Cockpit of the Revolution, The War for Independence in New Jersey.* (Princeton: Princeton University Press). Title.
[282] Ibid. 114.
[283] Ibid. 115.
[284] Force, *Archives*, 5th Ser, Vol. 1.14-15; 5th Ser, Vol.2, 1566.
[285] Ibid.17.

Washington strove to reduce the uneasiness of the New Jersey Militia and the fears of the citizenry. He also hoped to improve his own position in New York. Releasing the Militia would remove troops with short-term enlistments and hopefully aid in obtaining long-term levees. He mentions to General Livingston that "I have been the more induced to dismiss the Militia, that the new levees (or six months' men) maybe forwarded as soon as possible." He encouraged General Livingston to support and promote this action.[286]

William Livingston

In seeking his assistance General Washington was endeavoring to gain the aid of one of the most influential members of the New Jersey leadership. William Livingston was born in Albany, New York in November 1723. A graduate of Yale University he was admitted to the New Jersey Bar in 1748. William was a publisher and later a member of the Continental Congress. He was appointed commander of the New Jersey Militia. Later he would be the first governor of the State, serving from 1776-1790.[287] General Livingston replied to his Commander-in-Chief, "Everything in my power shall be carefully attended to for the publick good."[288] The effort to secure the region against internal and external enemies was a strategic necessity. Releasing the Militia from New York and dispatching Pennsylvania Associators to the Flying Camp aided in stabilizing the area.

Upon General Hugh Mercer's arrival in New Jersey the command of the Flying Camp and the militias evolved to him. He was tasked to protect New Jersey against invasion and insurgency. One of his first critical tasks was to secure the cooperation and support of General Livingston. He would have to provide the militia troops to serve until the Flying Camp forces arrived. A positive working relationship was established between the two officers. They jointly planned for the "posts and disposition of troops so that all ferries and likely landing places" were secured.[289] In rapid time a "total of 2000 Jersey Militia" troops were raised to defend the province until relief arrived. [290] General Mercer faced numerous difficulties in gathering and retaining forces and supplies in New Jersey. Dissatisfaction and worry among the local militia forces presented him with difficult command problems. On July 8th he wrote to General Washington about his inspection of

---

[286] Ibid.

[287] Jerry Kail. *Who Was Who During the American Revolution*. 208.

[288] Force, *Archives*, 5th Ser, Vol. 1. 18.

[289] Waterman. *With Sword and Lancet*. 112.

[290] Ibid. 113.

Bergen Neck and the militia posted there, commanded by a Colonel Ford. Of the Colonel's command he says "His force amounts to no more than three hundred and fifty, and those begin to be dissatisfied at remaining on duty, while the militia of the neighborhood are dismissed."[291]

In early July General Mercer's force in New Jersey consisted of local militia members. The Pennsylvania militia was on the march but wouldn't arrive in significant numbers until late in the month. Released from service in New York, the New Jersey troops returned home but remained unhappy with the situation. The annual harvest was due and the farmers were anxious to get their crops in. Failing to do so would dramatically affect their families and their existence. On July 9th, General Mercer noted in a letter to his commander-in-chief "they [New Jersey militia] begin to be so anxious to return to their harvest, under the apprehension of their families being without support, if they continue longer, that I have permitted a draught from each company to be discharged-about two hundred in all, and have assured the others they shall be relived when the *Pennsylvania* militia arrive, ten or twelve days hence the harvest, I am told, will be secured; when it is so, the militia will return to duty with Pleasure, and in the meantime will assemble at the first summons."[292]

The following day, Samuel Tucker, the President of the Provincial Congress, wrote to echo the concerns of the farmers over their harvest. The loss of labor on the farms due to militia service was seen to "have greatly drained us of men, at a time when the grain (the support of the Colony) is in imminent danger of being neglected and lost." He praises the news that the "*Pennsylvania* Militia was to march to our assistance." He states "while we enjoy" the opportunity to oppose the enemy we hoped to have the chance of "dismissing our Militia for the present in order that they may save and secure their grain, already suffering."[293] The fear of invasion was being overshadowed by the fear of starvation. The need to bring in the crops was of immense concern to the people of New Jersey. General Mercer's willingness to aid in accomplishing the task helped achieve the essential need.

On July 14th, General Mercer reported the arrival of "four hundred of the *Pennsylvania* rifle battalion" (Colonel Samuel Mile's command). He expected to relieve more of the New Jersey militia, as further reinforcements arrived. [294] On the 16th he notes "The clamor of the Militia to get to their harvest has obliged me to discharge many." [295] He was optimistic about protecting his region with the remaining troops and the soon to arrive Pennsylvanians. By July 20th General Mercer was telling John Hancock that "I have relieved with the troops sent from *Pennsylvania* all of the Militia of New Jersey… to enable them to secure their harvest. When that is effected, they will again cheerfully give their assistance." [296]

There was displeasure with the efforts to secure New Jersey. On July 9th, Samuel Tucker, expressing concerns over the burden being imposed, wrote to John Hancock "…we seem to be called upon to make provision for the entire defence of our own shore…" and "our funds are very inadequate." Enquiring about the support the

---

[291] Force, *Archives*, 5th Ser, Vol. 2. 120.
[292] Force, *Archives*, 5th Ser, Vol. 1. 140.
[293] Force, *Archives*, 5th Ser, Vol. 1. 172
[294] Force, *Archives*, 5th Ser, Vol. 2. 328.
[295] Ibid. 370.
[296] Ibib. 470.

Continental Congress was to provide, he reflects that the State was providing for the "defence of *New-York*" while the "Flying Camp is to protect" New Jersey. Believing that "provision would be made by the Continental Congress "for supplies and pay for the Camp. Mister Tucker added, "we contribute, to the defence of *New-York,* of *Boston,* of *Virginia,* of the *Carolinas.* When we are pressed by the stroke of war in our turn, are we alone to sustain the burden?"[297] The State leadership resented supporting the war elsewhere while feeling they were left to face the enemy alone. This disgruntled opinion would appear again, affecting the armies in New Jersey.

On July 16th General Washington, needing more troops, ordered two thousand militiamen in the Flying Camp to New York. His call corresponds with the desire of Congress, expressed in its resolution of that date. New Jersey's leadership agreed to release the troops. On July 18th the state convention issued "*An Ordinance for detaching two-thousand of the Militia-.*" which outlined the transfer of troops and their replacement with remaining militia forces. The arrangements directed that the new levy of replacements comprise "four battalions, consisting of thirty Companies of sixty four non-commissioned officers and privates, under the command of a Brigadier-General." The replacements were to "continue in service for the space of one calendar month, computing from the time of their joining the Flying Camp, unless sooner discharged." Each soldier was to "come equipped with a good Musket with a Bayonet...,a Tomahawk, a Cartouch-box, Blanket, Canteen, and Knapsack." The ordinance closes with an appeal to the soldiers," Remember, the hour is approaching which will in all human probability, decide the fate of *America*-... Life, liberty, and property, all await the issue of the present struggle. Arise, then, and exert yourselves!"[298] The Brigadier General selected for command of this levy was Philemon Dickinson [Dickerson].[299]

The Militia's early release from service in New York [July 5th] was a short lived repose for the troops. General Mercer's efforts to raise forces in the area were hampered by the call upon his ranks to meet the pressing needs in New York. The only accomplishment was the successful completion of the harvest. For the Militia it was a period of march and counter-march, mustering in, only to quickly be discharged and then being again recalled to serve. The impact upon the condition and morale of these citizen soldiers was injurious to the men and harmful to the army.

By mid-July, New Jersey had been called upon to provide nearly five thousand men for service. Congress then decided to augment the number of troops for the Flying–Camp. In a July 22nd letter to the Convention of New Jersey, John Hancock asked for three additional battalions of Militia.

> The Congress, taking into consideration the strength of our enemies and the force destined for the attack of *New-York*, have come to a resolution to increase the Flying Camp. For this purpose, I have it in charge to request that you immediately augment your quota to the Flying Camp with three battalions of Militia, in addition to those formerly desired by Congress, and send them, with all possible dispatch, to join the Flying Camp. The battalions are to be officered, paid, and provided, agreeable to former resolutions of Congress for establishing said Camp.

---

[297] Force, *Archives,* 5th Ser, Vol. 1. 138-139.
[298] Force, *Archives,* 4th Ser, Vol. 6. 1650.
[299] Force, *Archives,* 5th Ser, Vol. 2. 909.

I have the honor to be, gentlemen, your most obedient and very humble servant.

John Hancock, President [300]

The letter was received on July 25th. After its reading to the gathered assembly an order was put forth "That a Letter be written to Congress, informing that [the] Convention had ordered two thousand of its Militia to be detached pursuant to the late requisition [July 16th Congressional resolution] of Congress, which are to be renewed monthly."[301]

Compliance with the new Congressional request of was not easily obtained. Some serious political legwork and arm-twisting was required. Richard Stockton, a New Jersey State Delegate to the Congress visited the state prior to the issuance of the new request. In correspondence with Thomas Jefferson on July 19th, he relates his efforts to convince the State officials to support the Flying Camp. He had proposed the furnishing of 2,000 men by the state. He noted "they alleged their reasons against the measure which I expected, to wit, their having furnished their full proportion. " Mr. Stockton appears to allude that as the result of his urging they assured him they would comply with the request. [302]

New Jersey's militia system was a failure and imposed a burden that could not be effectively dealt with. As early as July 24th the State Convention had established a committee "to draft a Bill for amending the Militia Ordnance."[303] On August 2nd "the draft for amending the Militia Ordnance was read a second time, and referred to further consideration."[304] Substantial changes in the Militia system would appear as the result of the efforts to support General Mercer. To support the Flying Camp, on August 11th the Convention enacted an ordinance for "the immediate detaching of one-half of the Militia of this State to join the Flying Camp." It established that "all able-bodied men, without exception, in this State, between the ages of sixteen and fifty, be immediately enrolled by the Captains of the Militia in whose Districts they live, into their several companies." Half of the Militia was to be called into immediate service to be relieved by the other half on a monthly basis. To ensure that every serving soldier was completely equipped the arms

[300] Force, *Archives*, 5th Ser, Vol. 1. 495.
[301] Force, *Archives*, 4th Ser, Vol. 6. 1653.
[302] Julian P Boyd, Lyman H Butterfield, and Mira R Bryan, Eds. *The Papers of Thomas Jefferson, Volume 1, 1760 –1776.* (Princeton: Princeton Univ. Press, 1950), 467- 468.
[303] Force, *Archives*, 4th Ser, Vol. 6. 1653.
[304] Ibid. 1657.

and equipage of the standby units were to be collected. As the units rotated each month the weapons and equipment would be transferred as needed. [305]

Writing to General Washington on August 12th, William Livingston supplied that the "Militia, without exception, [is] to be immediately called out, and join the Flying Camp. That will be formed into thirteen battalions and are to remain on service one month. The two thousand men for the Flying Camp, under General *Dickerson* [Dickinson] are in great forwardness, and (although very little acquainted with their duty) might answer a valuable purpose in *New-York*... especially as their places will be soon filled by the half of the Militia now raised." [306]

General Mercer's August 20th Return (see Figure 4) reflects the presence of nine New Jersey Militia regiments, totaling 1375 troops under his command. The addition of the militia proved critical to strengthening the Flying Camp. In the return of October 8th, Mercer reports that ten regiments with a total of 3127 New Jersey militiamen are present for duty; an increase of 1752 troops. The militiamen accounted for 52% of the total strength recorded on the return (see Figure 5).

A General Return of the Army in New-Jersey, under the command of the Hon. Hugh Mercer, Esq., Brigadier-General, in the service of the American States, Perth-Amboy.

REGIMENTS.	Colonels	Lieut-Colonels	Majors	Captains	First Lieutenants	Sec'd Lieutenants	Ensigns	Chaplains	Adjutants	Quartermasters	Paymasters	Surgeons	Mates	Sergeants	Drums and Fifes	Priv's fit for duty	Sick	On Furlough	Deserted	Total	Total Officers and Privates	WHERE STATIONED.	FROM WHAT STATES AND WHAT TROOPS.
Colonel Shipman's	1	1	1	5	5	3	5	-	1	1	-	-	-	21	8	158	4	-	-	162	214	South-Amboy	Jersey Militia
Colonel Patterson's	1	1	1	8	8	8	8	1	1	1	1	1	1	32	15	309	89	-	-	398	-	Perth-Amboy	Delaware Flying-Camp
Colonel Denne's	1	-	1	6	6	3	2	-	1	1	-	1	-	14	6	138	6	5	-	149	-	Ditto	Jersey Militia
Colonel Somers's	1	-	1	3	3	1	3	-	1	1	-	1	-	22	5	74	6	-	-	80	-	Ditto	Ditto
Total at Amboy	3	1	3	17	17	12	13	1	3	3	1	3	1	68	26	521	101	5	-	627	799		
Colonel Chambers's	1	-	1	4	4	1	4	-	1	1	-	1	-	17	6	207	4	3	-	214		Woodbridge	Jersey Militia
Colonel Dick's	1	-	1	5	3	-	5	-	1	1	-	-	-	17	5	94	6	-	-	100		Ditto	Ditto
Colonel Seeley's	1	1	1	6	6	3	5	-	1	1	-	-	-	18	8	145	12	2	-	159		Ditto	Ditto
Total at Woodbridge	3	1	3	15	13	4	14	-	3	3	-	2	-	52	19	446	22	5	-	473	605		
Lieut. Colonel Lawrance's	-	-	-	3	3	3	2	-	-	-	-	-	-	9	3	98	-	-	-	98		Elizabeth-Town	Penn. Flying-Camp
Colonel Thomas's	1	1	1	8	8	-	6	1	1	-	1	1	-	30	9	265	-	-	-	265		Ditto	Jersey Militia
Colonel Ford's	1	-	1	7	8	-	7	-	1	1	1	1	1	25	12	278	-	-	-	278		Ditto	Ditto
Colonel Beaver's	1	1	1	4	5	-	3	-	1	1	-	1	-	15	6	145	-	-	-	145		Ditto	Ditto
Total at Elizabeth-Town	3	2	3	22	24	3	18	1	3	3	-	3	2	79	30	786	-	-	-	786	982		
Colonel Moore's	1	1	1	6	6	6	4	1	1	1	-	1	-	17	9	157	26	4	22	209	264	Newark	Penn'a. Flying-Camp
Colonel Clotz's	1	1	1	7	7	7	6	-	-	-	-	1	-	25	7	314	28	2	4	348		Fort Lee	Ditto
Colonel Swope's	1	1	1	8	7	7	7	-	1	1	-	1	1	29	13	310	47	1	-	358		Ditto	Ditto
Colonel Watts's	1	1	1	8	8	8	8	1	1	1	-	1	1	32	9	362	101	2	-	465		Ditto	Ditto
Colonel Montgomery's	1	1	1	7	5	6	4	-	1	1	-	-	-	23	6	244	35	-	-	279		Ditto	Ditto
Colonel McAllister's	1	1	1	6	5	6	6	-	1	1	-	1	-	23	7	301	40	4	3	348		Ditto	Ditto
Colonel Baxter's	1	-	-	5	7	7	3	1	1	1	-	1	-	25	5	289	36	8	10	343		Ditto	Ditto
Total at Fort Lee	6	5	5	41	39	41	34	2	5	5	-	4	2	157	47	1830	287	17	17	2141	2534		
Total of Troops	17	11	16	106	97	69	88	5	16	16	1	13	5	394	139	3888	440	39	39	4398	5398		Total Flying-Camp Militia.

N. B. There are four companies of *Maryland* inlisted Militia just come in that are not in the returns. They are to stay until the first of *December*.

Figure 4: Source: Force, *Archives*, Ser. 5, Vol. 1, 1079-1080.

---

[305] Ibid. 1661-62.
[306] Force, *Archives*, 5th Ser, Vol. 2. 909-910.

A General Return of the Army in New-Jersey, under the command of the Honourable Hugh Mercer, Esq., Brigadier-General in the service of the American States, Perth-Amboy, October 8, 1776.

REGIMENTS.	Colonels.	Lieut. Colonels.	Majors.	Captains.	First Lieutenants.	Second Lieut'nts.	Ensigns.	Chaplains.	Adjutants.	Quartermasters.	Paymasters.	Surgeons.	Mates.	Sergeants.	Drums and Fifes.	Privates, fit for duty.	Sick.	On furlough.	Deserted.	Total Privates.	Total Officers and Privates.	WHERE STATIONED.	FROM WHAT STATE.
Lieutenant-Colonel Ten...	-	1	2	4	5	5	4	-	1	1	-	1	-	13	9	108	25	1	5	139	185	South-Amboy	Pennsylvania Militia.
Colonel Patterson	1	-	1	7	6	6	5	1	1	1	1	1	1	27	12	268	74	-	-	342	-	Perth-Amboy	Delaware Flying-Camp.
Colonel Moore	1	-	1	8	8	8	7	-	1	1	-	1	-	26	8	231	51	5	24	311	-	do.	Pennsylvania do.
Colonel McCalister	1	-	1	9	8	7	8	1	2	2	-	2	-	35	8	369	61	8	-	438	-	do.	do.
Colonel Clotz	-	-	1	3	3	3	2	-	-	1	-	-	-	10	2	103	18	-	4	125	-	do.	do.
Colonel Read	-	1	-	3	3	2	2	-	-	-	-	1	-	8	4	98	10	1	-	109	-	do.	Jersey Militia.
Colonel Ellis	1	1	2	5	5	-	4	1	1	-	1	-	-	22	2	113	19	1	3	136	-	do.	do.
Colonel Shipman	1	1	1	9	8	8	5	1	1	-	-	-	-	1	-	246	-	-	-	246	-	do.	do.
Colonel Allison	1	1	2	4	4	4	2	1	1	-	-	-	-	15	1	92	13	2	-	107	-	do.	Pennsylvania do.
Colonel Savitz	-	-	-	2	2	1	2	-	-	1	-	-	-	6	4	50	-	-	-	50	-	do.	do.
Colonel Henderson	-	-	-	2	2	1	-	-	-	-	-	-	-	4	-	22	-	-	-	22	-	do.	do.
Total at Amboy	6	5	9	52	49	40	37	3	7	9	1	6	1	154	41	1592	246	17	31	1886	2306	Total at Perth-Amboy.	
Colonel Smith	1	-	1	4	4	-	4	-	1	1	-	-	-	15	7	193	25	3	-	221	-	Woodbridge	Jersey Militia.
Colonel Potter	1	1	2	6	6	6	6	-	-	1	1	-	-	25	12	138	39	2	1	180	-	do.	do.
Colonel Holmes	1	1	2	5	4	5	3	1	1	-	1	-	-	20	8	152	16	-	-	168	-	do.	do.
Total at Woodbridge	3	2	5	15	14	11	13	1	2	3	-	2	-	60	27	483	80	5	1	569	727	Total at Woodbridge.	
Lieutenant-Col. Lawrence	-	-	-	2	2	2	2	-	1	-	-	-	-	7	2	65	7	-	1	73	-	Elizabeth-Town	Pennsyl'a Flying-Camp.
Colonel Slough	-	1	2	5	5	4	4	-	1	1	-	-	-	15	10	171	-	-	-	171	-	do.	do. Militia.
Colonel Drake	1	-	1	9	7	7	7	-	1	1	-	-	-	33	12	368	-	-	-	368	-	do.	Jersey Militia.
Colonel Smith	1	-	2	10	7	7	7	-	1	1	-	1	1	35	8	405	52	8	13	478	-	do.	do.
Colonel Mettela	1	1	-	4	4	3	3	-	1	1	-	1	-	16	8	189	-	-	-	189	-	do.	do.
Total at Elizabeth-Town.	3	3	5	30	25	23	23	-	5	4	-	3	1	106	40	1198	59	8	14	1279	1550	Total at Elizabeth-Town.	
Colonel Nelson	1	1	2	6	6	-	6	1	1	-	-	-	-	18	10	236	14	6	-	256	310	New-Ark	Jersey Militia.
Colonel Swope	1	1	1	8	8	7	8	-	1	1	-	1	1	30	14	314	32	1	12	359	-	Fort Constitution	Pennsyl'a Flying-Camp.
Colonel Cunningham	1	-	1	3	8	-	1	-	1	-	-	-	-	12	1	121	13	4	-	138	-	do.	do.
Colonel Montgomery	-	1	1	7	7	6	6	-	1	-	-	-	-	24	5	224	44	1	36	305	-	do.	do.
Colonel Watt	1	-	1	6	7	7	7	-	-	-	-	-	-	27	8	368	63	-	4	435	-		
Total at Fort Constitution.	3	2	4	24	30	20	22	1	3	-	-	2	1	93	28	1027	152	6	52	1237	1470	Total at Fort Constitution.	
Total number	16	14	27	131	129	99	105	5	17	21	1	15	3	444	155	4644	576	103	103	5366	6548	At the different posts.	

Figure 5: Source: Force, *Archives,* Ser. 5, Vol. 2, 941-942.

Burden of the Few

Many of New Jersey's citizens sacrificed greatly to support the revolution. Thousands of men responded to the call to serve. Yet, dissent, disillusionment, and disregard caused many more to forego either initial service or a return to arms. The difficulty of mustering the troops needed is revealed in a July 24th letter from General Washington, sent to the New Jersey Convention. He reflects that General Heard's New Jersey Brigade was under strength, consisting of approximately 1300 rank and file; or a shortage of nearly 750 soldiers. The Convention responded in saying that efforts were underway to fill the gaps in the line. Still, by November 3rd, records reveal the Brigade had 1537 troops available, still a shortage. [307]

The Army's reliance upon the service of militia forces created grave concerns among the leadership. After the Battle of Long Island, General Washington called upon the Congress to provide for a regular army. On September 16th, Congress "*Resolved, That, eighty-eight Battalions be inlisted as soon as possible, to serve during the present war.*" Each state was assigned a quota of troops to supply for the battalions. A bounty of "twenty Dollars" was to be given "to each Non-Commissioned Officer and Private soldier." Provision was also made "for granting Lands" as reward to those serving in the army. [308]

---

[307] Force, *Archives,* 5th Ser, Vol. 3. 502.

[308] bid.53-54.

John Hancock, in a September 24th letter, introduced to the States the Congressional resolutions regarding the new Army.... "they [Congress] have come to a determination to augment our Army, and to engage the troops to serve during the continuance of the war." He supported the decision to establish a regular army with several points on the shortcomings of the militias. "The many ill consequences arising from a short and limited inlistment...the heavy and enormous expense consequent upon calling forth the militia, the delaying attending their motions, and the difficulty of keeping them in camp, render it extremely improper to place our whole dependence" on the service of the militias. "Without a well-disciplines army, we can never expect success against veteran troops; and it is totally impossible we should ever have a well-disciplined army unless our troops are engaged to serve during the war."[309] The citizen soldier, the militias, the minutemen were all gallant and valorous. But in this war they were facing an enemy that was arriving in great numbers and with vast experience, eclipsing the ability of these courageous volunteers to sustain the defense. The need for a more professional and capable standing army was obvious. It would be created in the form of the Continental Line.

The New Jersey Militia shared the same difficulties noted by John Hancock. General Washington wrote to Hancock on November 30th, " I hoped we should have met with large and early succours by this time; but as of yet no great number of the Militia of this State [New Jersey] has come in, nor have I much reason to expect that considerable aid will be derived from the Counties in which enemy are."[310] The General was accurate in his view that no large units could gather and march under the gaze of the enemy. He was hopeful that at least some small number of men might come forth from the counties involved.

General Washington's December 1st letter to Governor Livingston expresses a tone of condemnation of the State's Militia.

> Unless my force is speedily augmented, it will be impossible for me to make a stand at this place [Brunswick], when the enemy advance, as I have not, including General Williamson's Militia (say one thousand) more than four thousand men. The Militia of the Counties of *Morris* and *Sussex* turn out slowly and reluctantly; whether owing to the want of officers of spirit to encourage them, or your summons not being regularly sent to them, I cannot say; but I have reason to believe there has been a deficiency in both cases. Designing men have been purposely sent among them, to influence some and intimidate others; and except gentlemen of spirit and character will appear among them, and rouse them, little can be expected."[311]

On December 16th the General wrote to the Pennsylvania Council of Safety, "I am glad to find the Militia of the eastern parts of your Province, the lower parts of *Jersey*, and the *Delaware* Counties, are turning out with proper spirit." He adds a belated plea in a post-script, "P.S. I beg you will by all means facilitate and encourage the recruting

---

[309] Ibid. 209-210.
[310] Ibid. .919
[311] Ibid. 1027

service, for on that everything depends."[312] The Militia's failure to respond and serve contributed to the negative view of relying upon those forces.

General Nathanael Greene alludes to the "folly of short inlistments" in a letter to Governor Cook, dated December 4th. He writes, "The time for which the five months men were engaged expired at this critical period. Two Brigades left us at *Brunswick* notwithstanding the enemy were within two hours march and coming on." He relates the efforts being made to "draw our force together." Praising the Pennsylvania units that "turn out with great spirit" he notes "the *Jersey* Militia behaves scurvily, and I fear are not deserving the freedom we are contending for."[313]

George Washington clearly presents his views on the use of militia troops in a December 5th letter to John Hancock. While mentioning several examples when adequate militia forces failed to appear he comments," These, among ten thousand other instances, might be added to show the disadvantages of short inlistments, and the little dependence upon Militia in times of real danger." He continues, "my first wish is, that Congress may be convinced of the imporpriety of relying upon the Militia, and the necessity of raising a larger standing army than what we have voted." The General felt the Army would be best served by "having nothing to do with Militia unless in cases of extraordinary exigency." [314] He presented a number of reasons for the inadequacy of the militia response and its poor performance. The General appreciated the burden borne by these citizen soldiers, who were being called upon to serve with little know-how and less skill for military affairs. He reflects in a letter of December 12th to "Governour Trumbill" that "every thing must depend upon the regular force we can bring into the field in the spring; for I find, from fatal experience, that Militia serve only to delude us." [315]

Governor Livingston, of New Jersey, expressed little confidence in the militia of his state in his reply to General Washington on December 9th. He wrote "I shall be ready to call …the militia…but whether they will obey the order, God only knows; and they will be worth but little if they do, I experimentally know." [316] The Governor had lost faith in his own militia, which he had once commanded. His experimental knowledge of the capabilities and performance of his troops was based on hard experience, sad as it seems. A letter from Colonel Joseph Reed to John Hancock reflects the relative lack of Militia participation in New Jersey in the late part of 1776. He writes," The *Jersey* Militia are so few that no dependence can be placed upon them." The Pennsylvania militia

---

[312] Ibid. 1245.
[313] Ibid. 1071-1072.
[314] Ibid.1082-1083.
[315] Ibid. 1186.
[316] Ibid. 618.

troops "were very confused, the time not having admitted of any arrangement." [317] Colonel Reed's comments vividly illustrate the inadequate numbers of militia responding and the insufficient training and organization given to these forces.

The strain placed upon the militia had telling effects on the Army's performance. Large numbers of men were called out in New Jersey. All males between 16-50 years of age had been required to participate. But the available pool of men was greatly limited by existing factors. Significant numbers of potential recruits were Tories, opposed to the revolution. Other men were pacifists, many being Quakers who were unwilling to fight for religious reasons. A number of the citizenry were unaligned and preferred to remain detached from service to either side. The remaining who responded to the repeated calls carried a heavy burden. Some retreated from service while others held the course. We owe a deep debt to those who stood these trials and tribulations.

March and Hold

General Mercer was able to secure his area of command and provide support to General Washington's forces in New York. The State Militia aided in controlling key points, and along with the Flying Camp components, defended New Jersey against an early enemy incursion. Troops were placed at several locations: Powles (Paulos) Hook, Bergen Point, Bergen Neck, and Bergen Heights; all being posts which guarded the approaches from Staten Island. As the Flying Camp levees arrived garrisons were placed at South Amboy, Woodbridge, Newark, Hoboken, Blazing Star Ferry, and later at Fort Lee (Fort Constitution).

The primary mission was to protect and control New Jersey, and thus the approaches to the middle states. Never satisfied with a purely defensive role, General Washington wanted to use Mercer's forces in surprise assaults against the enemy. With the Flying Camp not yet six weeks old, it was to use it in an enterprise against the British post at Blazing Star on Staten Island. Forces of the Connecticut Line, serving with the command at Powles Hook, were to conduct the raid. On July 18th three hundred men commanded by Major Thomas Knowlton were to assault the outpost. The expedition failed due to bad weather preventing the crossing of the straight between Staten Island and New Jersey. On October 15th another attempt was to use the Flying Camp forces against the British on Staten Island. New Jersey Militia men from Elizabethtown, Blazing Star Ferry, and Newark joined the attempt. Accompanying them was the Delaware Flying

---

[317] Ibid. 1107

Camp unit of Colonel Samuel Patterson. Additional troops from the Maryland contingent of the Flying Camp accompanied the force. [318]

The 1776 invasion of New Jersey began with the capture of Fort Lee. The fight for control of the State would culminate with the Battles of Trenton and Princeton. New Jersey's finale with the Flying Camp appears in a postscript to General Washington's letter to John Hancock, of December 1st, "*P.S. Half after one o'clock, P.M. – The enemy are fast advancing. Some of 'em are now in sight. All the men of the Jersey Flying Camp, under General Howe, being applied to have refused to continue longer in service.*" [319] The "Cockpit of the Revolution" was a forge which hardened the Americans, and especially New Jersey's sons, for the continued fight. The State made substantial contributions to the raising and service of the Flying Camp. It was a costly, difficulty, but eventually worthy effort.

---

[318] William H. Richardson. "Washington and the New Jersey Campaign of 1776." *Proceedings of the New Jersey Historical Society.*(April 1932), Vol. 50.no 2. page135-136,143.
[319] Force, *Archives,* 5th Ser, Vol.3. 1026-1027.

Operations in New Jersey[320]

---

[320] Henry B. Carrington. *Battle Maps and Charts of the American Revolution....*(Chicago: A.S. Barnes,1881) 302.

General Mercer's command included the short term attachment of some Connecticut regiments. As noted earlier, the 20th Connecticut Continental Regiment was used to mount an attack upon the British on Staten Island. Originally raised in January 1775, the Regiment was to be comprised of 650 members. Initially, it was commanded by Colonel Benedict Arnold, from January 1st 1775 to January 1st 1776. Colonel Arnold never appears to have assumed command of the unit; Lieutenant Colonel John Durkee fulfilled the role. [322]

The 20th Regiment, with other Connecticut units, marched for New York. It was stationed along with a second regiment at Paulus Hook, New Jersey under Mercer's command. While there, the most significant event the unit participated in was the July 18th abortive action against Staten Island. Six days earlier, on July 12th "at a Council of War, held at Head-Quarters...his Excellency General Washington...proposed to the consideration of the Board a plan of a decent upon *Staten-Island* in different places." The idea was deemed unworkable by the gathered officers. "The General then proposed a Partisian Party, with a view to alarm the enemy and incourage our own Troops." Major Thomas Knowlton of the 20th Continental Regiment had "reconnoitred the Island" and with General Mercer "deem such a surprise practicable." [323] It was agreed that a raid could be conducted and on July 16th General Washington sent orders for such to General Mercer.

Thomas Knowlton was a key figure in these events. Now considered one of Connecticut's Revolutionary War heroes, Knowlton was an energetic officer with a fondness for ranger tactics. He was born November 22nd, 1740 in West Boxford, Massachusetts. In the French and Indian War he enlisted, at age 15, in Captain John Durkee's Company. He served heroically and was promoted to Lieutenant in 1760. After the war he became a gentleman farmer in Connecticut and served in the local government. When news of Lexington reached his home he "grabbed his musket and powder horn and joined his militia company." He was elected as the Captain of his company. Combining with several other militia units the Companies formed the Fifth

---

[321]Stanley L Ralph. *Nutmeg* (State Cantata), (2003) ,www. netstate.com/state/symb/song/ct-the nutmeg. 8 August 2005.

[322] Fred A. Berg. *Encyclopedia of Continental Army Units: Battalions, Regiments and Independent Corps.* (Harrisburg PA: Stackpole Books, 1972), 35.

[323] Force, *Archives*, 5th Ser, Vol. 1. 224.

Regiment Connecticut Militia. Captain Knowlton and his men served at the Battle of Bunker Hill, forming the rear guard covering the American retreat. Congress, recognizing his bravery, promoted him to the rank of Major. The 1776 reorganization of the American Army placed him in the 20th Continental Regiment with his old commander, then Lieutenant Colonel Durkee. [324]

On July 16th, Hugh Mercer sent General Washington the plans for the assault upon Staten Island. The Connecticut Regiment, under "Major Knowlton to march next, with two hundred and fifty of his regiment, fifty *Pennsylvania* Riflemen, and fifty Militia, towards the *Blazing Star.*" [325] On July 18th, General Mercer advised his Commander-in-Chief that preparations were complete. He notes, " I intend to prosecute the plan... we hope to defer the attack till break of day, ... From our being able to discover no unusual movements in the enemy's quarter, it is presumable they have on hint of being surprised." [326] The same day he ordered Major Knowlton; "you are to march your party of three hundred men to attack the enemy's post at *New Blazing Star."* He provided specific directions for the movement and the assault; instructing the Major about the handling of prisoners and to "use the people on the Island with civility, unless they appear in arms." Here is an early example of revolutionary strategy and practice regarding civil populations in a war zone. These practices became the key foundations of later political -military strategy for succeeding revolutionaries. The General's letter provides an example of military-political tactics.

> Sir: You are to march your party of three hundred men to attack the enemy's post at *New Blazing- Star.* If possible, have your men near the enemy before break of day. While you attempt to surprise the enemy, be careful that you are not discovered. Have a small guard advance, and if they come unexpectedly on a sentinel, endeavor to sieze his arms and prevent giving an alarm by firing, unless the enemy is prepared and formidable. Let a profound silence be observed during the march, and keep your men in *Indian* file, about one pace asunder. If oblidged to appear openly against the enemy, have some of your best Riflemen on your flanks, with orders to gain, if possible, the flanks of the enemy. If they have artillery, a sudden push is necessary to gain possession of them. Should you be successful enough to take any of the *British* troops prisoners, secure them well and treat them with humanity. Use the people on the Island with civility, unless they appear in arms. As soon assist is light, send out flanking parties to secure you from surprise. I am, sir, your most humble servant,   Hugh Mercer. [327]

On July 19th, General Mercer had the unpleasant task of informing his Commander that the enterprise against Staten Island had floundered. He tells that "the wind and tide being against them, the boats could not be soon brought to us, as we expected. In the mean time the weather became to tempestuous to venture the *Sound* in scows." He admits that the assault "cannot be renewed till we have more forces here, nor would it be prudent to attempt any surprise for some days, as our motions are

---

[324] *LT.COL. Thomas Knowlton Connecticut's Forgotten Hero.*[electronic edition]. Connecticut Society of the Sons of the American Revolution. http://www.ctssar.org. October 2004.
[325] Force, *Archives*, 5th Ser, Vol. 1. 370.
[326] Ibid. 413.
[327] Ibid. Letter from General Mercer to Major Knowlton. 413.

probably communicated to the enemy." [328] The element of surprise had been lost as time and tide had not waited favorably upon Mercer's venture.

Later, Colonel Durkee's Regiment along with Major Knowlton, marched to New York arriving there the day before the Battle of Long Island. The Major, along with one hundred troops was posted at Flatbush Pass. On August 10th Lieutenant Colonel Durkee was promoted to Colonel and full command of the 20th Continental Regiment. Major Knowlton was promoted to Lieutenant Colonel in the regiment.[329] Later, he would be detached from the regiment to form a unit of Connecticut rangers. Thomas Knowlton was killed in action at the battle of Harlem Heights on September 16th, 1776. [330]

Virginia
"carry me back..."[331]

The Congressional committee appointed to develop measures for increasing the Flying Camp had delivered their report on July 20th. As recommended, Congress "resolved that "Brigadier-General *Lewis* be directed to order two Battalions of the Continental Troops, in *Virginia,* to march, with all possible despatch, to the Flying –Camp, in *New Jersey.*" [332] President of the Congress John Hancock wrote to Patrick Henry, Governor of Virginia on July 22nd:

> Sir: The Congress having directed General *Lewis* to order two battalions of continental troops, in the State of *Virginia ,* to march immediately to the Flying Camp, in *New Jersey,* under the command of General *Mercer* , I have it in charge to inform you that should you have reason to apprehend an invasion of that State, and in consequence there for call forth an equal number of the Minute-men or Militia, the Congress have resolved, that while in service they shall be in Continental pay. [333]

The same courier carried a similar letter to Brigadier General Andrew Lewis, commanding the Continental forces in Virginia. It reads:

> Sir: As it is impossible to ascertain the strength, or the force destined for the attack of *New-York,* it is incumbent on us to prepare to defend ourselves against any number of troops that may be ordered against that place. For this purpose the Congress have judged it necessary to augment the Flying Camp. I have it therefore in command to direct, that, immediately on the receipt of this, you order two battalions of the continental troops in the State of *Virginia* to march with all possible dispatch to the Flying Camp in *New Jersey,* under the command of General *Mercer.*
> The state of our affairs, and the hourly expectation of the arrival of the foreign troops, render it absolutely necessary that the troops should be sent forward with the greatest expedition. [334]

---

[328] Ibid. 443.

[329] Ibid. 1644.

[330] Boatner. 586.

[331] James Bland. *Carry Me Back to Old Virginny,*(1878). www. netstate.com/state/symb/song/va-carry-me-back. 8 August 2005.

[332] Force, *Archives,* 5th Ser, Vol. 1. 1586.

[333] Ibid, 494.

[334] Ibid. 494-495.

On August 3rd, John Page, President of the Virginia Convention, wrote from Williamsburg in response to John Hancock's letter of July 22nd. He acknowledged the request of Congress and reported that the Virginia leadership, "have reason to apprehend an invasion, and have therefore ordered a number of Minute-men and Militia into duty, to supply the want of our two regiments ordered to the *Jerseys.*" The state leadership considered the addition of the militia an inadequate substition for the "Regulars."[335]

On the same day, General Andrew Lewis replied to the President of Congress on the issue.

> Sir: By yesterday's post I was honored with the order of Congress, by which I am to send to the Flying Camp in *New-Jersey*, two battalions of the Continental troops in this State. This shall be done as expediously as in my power, though, from the dispersed condition of the troops in affording a general protection, it cannot be so soon as I could wish. Shall this State be attacked by a large body of the enemy in the absence of those two battalions, I shall not be able to give them the reception I could wish. With our whole force, (as it now stands,) it would be difficult, considering the many rivers that give them entrance to any or as many parts of this country as they could wish. Another circumstance, too, will (I doubt) weaken us: the first and Second Battalions were inlisted for no more than twelve months, which is nearly expired, and they have as yet refused to inlist for a longer time. I shall use my best endeavours to have them inlisted on Continental establishment. I shall do myself the honor to write you more fully the next post. [336]

Andrew Lewis was born in Donegal, Ireland in 1720. Immigrating to the Americas, he later served as a Major, under the command of George Washington, in the Ohio campaigns of 1754-55. He was later an officer in the Virginia Militia, a Justice of the Peace, and a representative in the colonial legislature. In Lord Dunmore's War he led the forces defeating the Indians at the Battle of Point Pleasant. He was a member of the Revolutionary Colonial Conventions in 1775. He became a Brigadier General in the Continental Army in 1776, commanding the forces in Virginia. He defeated the British under Lord Dunmore at Gwynn's Island in 1776. Resigning from the Army in 1777 he assumed a position on the State Executive Council. He died in Bedford County on September 26th, 1781. [337]

For the first time Virginians were to march in large numbers into the major fray. Yet, the effort would not be quick or appreciated by the troops. Discipline among the State troops was a problem which was further incensed in the summer of 1776. The morale among the First and Second regiments was seriously low. The men had announced they had no intention of reenlisting under the present command and circumstances. General Lewis used all of his persuasion and "best endeavours" to sway the troops into remaining in service. Additional bounties and personal appeals for the men "to seize the post of Honor" were extended. The results were mixed; the First Regiment, "almost to the man swallowed the bait." In the Second Regiment "not a man

---

[335] Ibid.736.
[336] Ibid. 736.
[337] Jerry Kail. *Who Was Who During the American Revolution.* 329.

stepped forward." Finally, it was the First and the Third Regiments which marched northwards to serve under General Washington. The Second Regiment was dissolved shortly thereafter. [338]

General Lewis wrote to John Hancock in early August (exact date is unknown but is between the 6th and 12th of the month). He informs him that the "First and Third Battalions" have been ordered "to march with all speed to the Flying Camp in the *Jerseys*." The Third Battalion, commanded by Colonel George Weedon, was stationed in Northern Virginia along the Potomac River so he expected it to arrive earlier. The First Regiment, commanded by Colonel Issac Read, was near its expiration date and several days had been needed to reenlist the regiment. General Lewis notes that the numbers were not complete but expected shortages would be rectified in a few days. He comments that "the officers of that battalion have shown a noble spirit in exerting themselves to the utmost in engaging the men on this occasion." He mentions that the regiment would "march next *Monday*." [339] The First Virginia Regiment left Williamsburg for New York on Tuesday, August 13th. [340]

On August 28th Congress was informed that "one of the Virginia Battalions was on the march to *New Jersey*" via Yorktown and Philadelphia. [341] The same day, John Hancock sent a letter to the battalion commander warning him to avoid Philadelphia due to the appearance of smallpox in the city. The Battalion was ordered to proceed directly to New Jersey.[342] On September 1st, General Washington sent orders to General Mercer that all men intended for the Flying Camp were to be sent to New York.[343] This directive applied to the Virginia regiments then on the march. In a following letter of September 8th, General Washington comments that he is "anxoius for the arrival of *Maryland* and *Virginia* troops," in New York. [344] In a subsequent correspondence on September 11th he notes he had received General Mercer's letters via Colonel Weedon. The Virginia Regiments' arrival in New York was a boost to the morale of General Washington's Army. A letter from Captain John Clinton of the Third Virginia Regiment reflects: "Great joy was expressed at our arrival and great things are expected of Virginians." [345]

The Return of the Army dated September 11th reveals Colonel Read's Regiment being assigned to General James Clinton's Brigade. The Regiment was composed of 505 rank and file and 82 officers and staff members. [346] The Return of the Army dated September 21st places the units in the area of King's Bridge, New York. It reflects the presence of Colonel Weedon's Third Virginia Regiment, with 602 rank and file and 98 officers and staff members. [347] The Virginians quickly found themselves engaged in combat against the British. Both regiments would participate in the Battle of Harlem Heights on September 16th. Three companies of the Third Virginia under Major Andrew Leitch, along with Lieutenant Colonel Thomas Knowlton's Connecticut Rangers, were involved in a foray beyond the American lines to locate the enemy. Both officers in

---

[338] .John E Selby. *The Revolution in Virginia 1775-1783*. (Williamsburg VA: Colonial Williamsburg Foundation,1988). 127-128.

[339] Force, *Archives*, 5th Ser, Vol. 1.1053.

[340] Ibid. 973.

[341] Ibid 1622.

[342] Ibid.1191.

[343] Force, *Archives*, 5th Ser, Vol. 2. 121.

[344] Ibid.240.

[345] Minnis, M. Lee. *The First Virginia Regiment of Foot 1775-1783* (Willow Bend Books, 1998). 19.

[346] Force, *Archives*, 5th Ser, Vol. 2. 327.

[347] Ibid.451.

command were mortally wounded in the engagement. Colonel Knowlton dying on the field while Major Leitch lingered till his death on October 1st. [348]

The Virginia regiments would remain with General Washington through the movement to White Plains and beyond to the Battle of Trenton. Though they were originally summoned to support the Flying Camp their service with such never matured. These hardy Virginians would suffer and serve with honor during the faithful period of late 1776.

---

[348] Minnis. 20.

Chapter 8
Glory Forgotten

It was decided to place the headquarters of the Flying Camp "at a place concentrical" to the posts that it commanded. [349]   General Mercer elected to post his command at [Perth] Amboy, New Jersey. Writing to General Washington on July 16th he states:

> Sir: I have just received a letter ... from Mr. Hancock. When I formerly mentioned *Brunswick,* as a proper place for the camp, my idea of the intention of raising and collecting an army here, was for the security of *Philadelphia* only; but as I find the design is equally to secure this Colony and *Pennsylvania* , or assist in the operations on the *New York* side, I am well satisfied that *Amboy* will in every view best fulfill that intention. [350]

The General's letter reports his choice of location for the Camp and illustrates the expanded role ascribed to his command. The security of New Jersey had assumed a larger prominence in General Washington's strategic plans. Also, the close availability of the troops to support his operations in New York was beneficial. In retrospect we can see the beginning of "mission creep" for General Mercer's Flying Camp. A circumstance probably not unwarranted under the situation but obviously not planned or provided for.

The August 20th "General Return of the Army in New Jersey" reflects a total of 5398 officers and privates under General Mercer's command. [351]   These were divided among four main locations; Amboy (799), Woodbridge (605), Elizabethtown (982), and Fort Lee (2534). The remainder was posted among smaller sites supported by the main locations. Eventually, the command would have troops stationed at locations stretching from Fort Lee in the north to Sandy Hook in central New Jersey.

A Strong Defense but a Faint Heart
...the Engineers

The defense of New Jersey necessitated the control of the crossings between the adversary's positions. The significance of these portals into New Jersey became more apparent as the campaign progressed. The construction of fortifications and emplacement of artillery was critical to the defense. Considering that the "best officered, drilled and equipped army in the world" was as little as 220 yards from the shore the significance of a stout defense is obvious. [352]

The following is a sidelight into the staffing of the Flying Camp and the involvement of French "soldiers of fortune" in the American revolt. A letter from   "Mr. Duboug to Dr. Franklin, [dated] Paris, March 24,1776" introduces the Chevalier de Kirmovan as "one of the best men your country can acquire. He has embraced its sentiments, and neither demands, nor has ambitions of obtaining, any rank until his zeal and talents have been experienced. He is willing to devote himself to all dangers, ... he appears to me well instructed in the military art."[353]   A second letter presenting the "Chevalier" to Benjamin Franklin appears from General Horatio Gates, dated June 23rd.

---

[349] Richardson. 121.
[350] Force, *Archives*, 5th Ser, Vol.1. 371.
[351] Ibid. 1079.
[352] Richardson. 122.
[353] Force, *Archives*, 4th Ser, Vol.6. 1726.

He introduces the gentleman, noting he had left "Old France on the 6th of April, and arrived about fourteen days ago at *Stonington.*" The "Chevalier" carried letters from Franklin and "Doctor Rush." General Gates comments that the man "professes being an engineer, and to have served all the last war with the *Turks* in that line." The General's letter was presented before the Board of War on June 28th. [354]

A report was sent forward to the Congress the same day. It stated that "Monsieur Le Chevalier de Kirmovan, having produced to the Board indubitable credentials of his … superior abilities in the art of war and particularly as an engineer" he would be welcomed to aid in the cause. It was recommended that he be referred to the Pennsylvania Committee of Safety to employ him in "planning and laying out the fortification agreed by Congress…" at Billingsport on the Delaware River. [355]

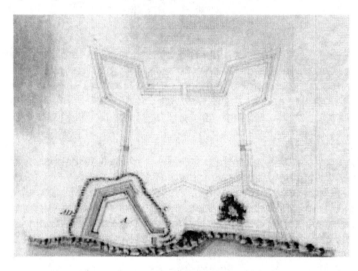

Plan and section of the Redoubt at Billingsport. LOC[356]

On July 4th the Pennsylvania Committee of Safety employed Kirmovan to lay out the fortifications at Billingsport. [357] A lightly held, unfinished redoubt was constructed on the site. It played a minor role during General Howe's Philadelphia campaign in October 1777. When the British attacked the position "the defenders spiked their guns, burned the barracks, and fled."[358] How much of a role Mons. Kirmovan had in developing the site is unknown. On July 16th the gentleman was "Appointed an engineer in the continental service, with the pay of 60 Dollars per month, and the rank of Lieutenant Colonel." He

[354] Ibid. 1004

[355] *A Century of Lawmaking for a New Nation.* Journals of the Continental Congress, Volume 5. (June 28th , 1776). HTTP://[Online]:http://memory.loc.gov/cgi-bin/querry/r?ammem/hlaw:@field(DOCID+@lit(jc00521)) 3 December 2004.

[356] Library of Congress, "Plans and Sections of the Redoubt at Billingsport and plan of the rebel fort marked yellow." Map Collection.1777?:The American Revolution and Its Era: Maps and Charts of North America and the West Indies,1750-1789.[Online] Available http://memory.loc.gov/cgi-bin/query/D?gmd:3:./temp/~ammem_rSCB::, Library of Congress, Washington DC. 6/6/05.

[357] Force, *Archives,* 4th Ser, Vol.6. 1300.

[358] Boatner. 77.

was "ordered to repair immediately to New Jersey" to be under the command of General Mercer. [359] Thus did the Flying Camp receive an Engineer.

The Chevalier de Kirmovan was joined in the Camp by another of his countrymen, Jacques Antoine de Franchessian, also as an engineer. It was to him that on July 20th the Congress had resolved that a "Brevet commission of Lieutenant Colonel be granted to … a Knight of the Order of St. Louis, an experienced officer in the French service, and who is well recommended in letters from abroad." An American, a Captain Samuel Davis was also assigned to serve as an assistant engineer. [360] Together they seem to have quickly started work on the defenses. Mons. de Kirmovan submitted a letter to Congress, received July 29th, which included "a plan and draughts." These were referred to the Board of War for consideration. [361]

The provision of qualified engineers emphasizes the defensive role assigned to General Mercer's command. This role is further enforced by the efforts to supply artillery to the command. The need for heavy guns to guard the approaches from New York and Staten Island was obvious. In early July, General Livingston had placed a Militia artillery unit with "four fieldpieces" at the Blazing Star Ferry. General Washington had supported the move and had dispatched an engineer to "erect some works for the security of these places." [362]

…the Artillery

General Mercer understood the need for strong defensive positions at the most likely assault points. The July 24th General Return for his command reports three companies of artillery were assigned. One was a Pennsylvania company consisting of two guns. There were two New Jersey companies with six guns total. General Mercer accounts for two guns at Newark, two at Elizabethtown, two at Woodbridge, and four at Amboy. This is a total of ten field pieces, apparently two guns were available that were not part of a specific artillery company. [363]

In a July 26th letter to Congress, General Mercer bemoans the failure of his pitifully few cannon to control the sea approaches and landings. He writes: "some shallops passing… yesterday afternoon brought on a cannonade. Our field-pieces did little or no execution… The enemy fired four, six, and twelve-pound shot very briskly for space of an hour; we lost one man… and two wounded. Some four or six pounders might be mounted… to answer very well against such vessels… Some such pieces as are mentioned above are to be had at *Philadelphia*… the engineer… is planning some works for securing… the location." [364] The General tasked his engineers to improve the fortifications at his positions. The need for heavy guns was obviously vital to the strength of the sites. His letter was received and read before the Congress on July 29th. It was dully ordered "that a number of four and six-pounders, not exceeding ten of each, be immediately sent to General Mercer to be mounted on the works he is now erecting; and

[359]. *A Century of Lawmaking for a New Nation*. Journals of the Continental Congress, Volume 5,(July 16th, 1776), HTTP://[Online]:http://memory.loc.gov/cgi-bin/querry/r?ammem/hlaw:@field(DOCID+@lit(jc00535)) 3 December 2004.

[360] Richardson.160.

[361] *A Century of Lawmaking for a New Nation*. Journals of the Continental Congress, Volume 5,(July 29th, 1776), HTTP://[Online]:http://memory.loc.gov/cgi-bin/querry/r?ammem/hlaw:@field(DOCID+@lit(jc00545)) 6 December 2004

[362] Waterman. 110.

[363] Force, *Archives*, 5th Ser, Vol.1. 55.

[364] Ibid.599

that the Council of Safety of *Pennsylvania* be requested to forward them to *Amboy,* in *New Jersey.*"[365] John Hancock wrote to the Council of Safety on July 31st. He directed that "ten six-pounders and an equal number of four-pounders" be forwarded to General Mercer. If not available in sufficient number whatever could be spared were to be sent.[366] The Council responded to the request and "Ordered that captain John Blewer procure and forward the Guns."[367]

...the Forts

General Washington assigned General Charles Lee the role of developing the defenses of the City and the Hudson River in February, 1776. Lee determined that the river was too deep and wide to be defended near the City. His opinion held sway until June when the decision was made to establish fortifications in the area of the upper York Island. [368] It was hoped that the defense of the Hudson River and New Jersey would be enhanced by the construction of two major forts. Forts Lee and Washington were built to anchor the ends of a defensive line of obstructions placed across the Hudson. Each was to include defensive works and artillery batteries. Additionally, a line of sunken vessels and *chevaux-de-frise* were placed across the river to impede river traffic.[369] Robert Yates, Chairman of the Secret Committee for obstructing the channel at Fort Washington relates in a letter of September 25th, "We've obtained two sloops, two brigs, and two large ships, for the purpose of obstructing the channel." [370] The design of the *chevaux-de-frise* used isn't known but an example of a type common to the period is provided below.

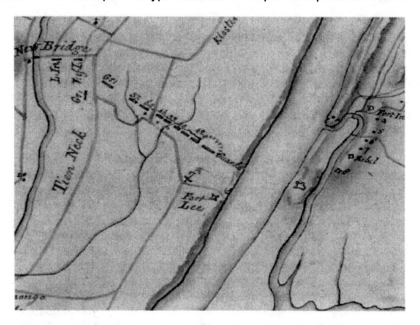

Plan of the country at and in the vicinity of Forts Lee and Independency.... LOC.[371]

---

[365] *A Century of Lawmaking for a New Nation.* Journals of the Continental Congress, Volume 5,(July 30th, 1776), http://memory.loc.gov/cgi-bin/query/r?ammem/hlaw:@field(DOCID+@lit(jc00546)):621

[366] Force, *Archives,* 5th Ser, Vol.1. 690

[367] Ibid.1303.

[368] William Paul Deary. *Toward Disaster at Fort Washington. November 1776.* (Ann Arbor: UMI, 1995). 14-16.

[369] Edward F DeLancey. *The Capture of Mount Washington November 16th, 1776, The Result of Treason.* New York, 1877. 8.

[370] Force, *Archives,* 5th Ser, Vol.3. 204.

[371] "Plan of the country at and in the vicinity of Forts Lee and Independency, showing the position of the British Army." Map Collection, 1776? :The American Revolution and Its Era: Maps and Charts of North America and

Example of Chevaux-de-frize

The site on the New York side of the river was named "Mount Washington" in 1776 and was invested with a series of defensive lines. The central bastion was actually known as "Fort Washington." [372] Designed by Colonel Rufus Putnam, Engineer in Chief, the Fort was an earthwork "star fort" composed of five bastions. No casements, barracks, or well were provided. It was basically a large, open, earthen fort. It was built in July 1776 by Pennsylvania units commanded by Brigadier General Thomas Mifflin; Colonel Robert Magaw's Fifth battalion and Colonel John Shee's Third battalion. Colonel Magaw would later be given command of the units located at Fort Washington (see below). [373]

the West Indies,1750-1789.[Online] Available http://memory.loc.gov/cgi-bin/query/D?gmd:2:./temp/~ammem_rSCB:: ::, Library of Congress, Washington DC. 6/6/05.
[372] DeLancey 7.
[373] Ibid.9.

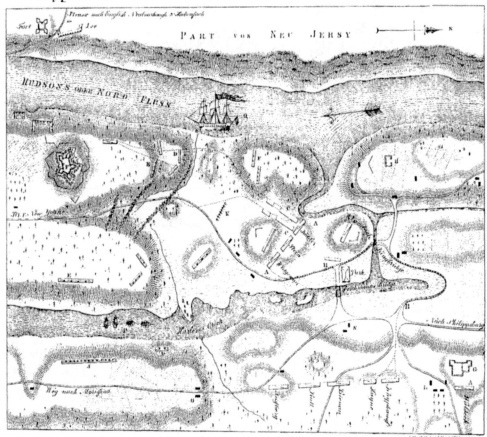

Map illustrating the assault upon Fort Washington[374]

       The obstructions proved ineffective in blocking the Royal Navy from advancing up the Hudson River. The British moved their vessels past the sites on several occasions. [375] The defenses on Mount Washington would also prove frail.   General Nathanael Greene was given command of forces in New Jersey in September, 1776. In a November 12th letter to John Hancock he expressed that "I expect General How will attempt to possess himself of Mount Washington but very much doubt whether he'll succeed....Our Troops are much fatigued with the Amazeing duty, but are generally in good Sprits."[376] Greene's belief that Howe would attack Mount Washington was echoed by General Washington. After the Battle of White Plains, in a November 6th letter to John Hancock, he writes "I think it highly probable, and almost certain, that he [General Howe] will make a descent with a part of his troops into *Jersey.*..... I expect the enemy will bend their force against *Fort Washington,* and invest it immediately. From some advices, it is an object that will attract their earliest attention." [377] Wise council and an astute conclusion on General Washington's part for ten days later, November 16th Howe's

[374] Ibid. illustrations.
[375] Boatner.381,386.
[376] Nathanael Greene, Vol 1, 349.
[377] Force, *Archives,* 5th Ser, Vol.3. 542-543.

British and German forces struck Washington's namesake fort. But the fort had not been abandoned and the resulting battle ended in a humiliating defeat for the Americans.

The loss of Fort Washington created doubts in the minds of senior military commanders and other leaders about George Washington's abilities as Commander-in-Chief. Much has been written on the matter and the resulting events. This forum will not serve to address the subject in detail. I refer readers to the work by Bruce Chadwick, *George Washington's War* for a start in learning more of the times, circumstances, and events surrounding General Washington and the American Army of 1776.[378]

After the fall of Fort Washington on November 16th, General Howe turned his attention to Fort Lee. During the same period that Fort Washington was constructed, General Mercer's Flying Camp troops had built Fort Lee on the summit of the Palisades, above the Hudson River.[379] Initially, New Jersey Militia built an artillery battery on the heights. Colonel Putnam then laid out the fortifications which comprised a square-bastioned earthwork and gun emplacements.[380] The General's August 20th Return of Forces shows there were 2534 troops assigned to Fort Lee.[381] By November 20th, the day of the assault, troops from the Flying Camp and the New Jersey Militia were there. General Nathanael Greene writes on December 4th, "The troops at Fort Lee were mostly of the Flying Camp, irregular and undisciplined. Had they obeyed orders, not a man would have been taken." [382]

The Americans had been warned of General Howe's maneuvers towards the New Jersey site. Time was barely sufficient to allow for the evacuation of the two thousand troops. The British attacked on November 20th capturing "twelve drunken Americans" in the fort and about 150 others in the vicinity. [383] General Howe's "Return of Prisoners" lists one Lieutenant, one Ensign, one Quartermaster, three surgeons and ninety-nine Privates captured. The losses of weapons and materiel were far more devastating to the cause. General Howe reports the capture of eighteen artillery pieces: five 32-pounders, three 24-pounders, two 6-pounders, two 3-pounders, and six mortals of various sizes. [384] The staggering loss of other stores included 432 tents, 400,000 rounds of ammunition, and a three month supply of provisions for 5000. [385]

...the Physicians

The heart of the Army, the soldiers, was always faint due to the losses of men from illness, disease, and injury. The provision of medical care was essential for the wellbeing of the troops. Among the physicians serving in the Army was William Shippen. Educated in Edinburgh, earning his medical degree in 1761, he was considered one of the finest of doctors in the colonies. Residing in Philadelphia he was active in advancing the study of medicine. He taught at the College of Philadelphia, and established various courses in specific practices.[386] In a letter of July 15th Dr Shippen was informed that Congress "this day appointed you Surgeon-general and Director of the Hospital for the

[378] Bruce Chadwick. *George Washington's War*. (Naperville Illionis:Sourcebooks,2004).
[379] DeLancey. 9.
[380] Robert B Roberts. *Encyclopedia of Historic Forts*, (New York: Macmillan Publishing Company, 1988). 511.
[381] Force, *Archives*, 5th Ser, Vol.3. 729.
[382] Ibid. 1071.
[383] Boatner. 381.
[384] Force, *Archives*, 5th Ser, Vol. 3.1058.
[385] von Muenchhausen. 5.
[386] Purcell. *Who Was Who in the American Revolution*. 442..

Flying –Camp and Militia in New Jersey, with the pay of four dollars a day." [387] His report of November 1st reflects the burden that sickness and injury placed upon him and the soldiers of the Flying Camp.

Amboy, 1st November 1776.
Enclosed is a return of the sick in my Hospitals. Besides these …in each regiment a number called sick …are under the care of the Regimental Surgeons, though there are no Regimental Hospitals.

A Return of the Sick in the Hospitals of Flying-Camp and Jersey Militia.

At Amboy, two Hospitals: Sick, 90; wounded, 7- total 97.
At Elizabeth-town: Sick, 54; wounded, 3; sick from Canada, 25 – total, 82.
At Fort Lee: Sick of our own, 75; wounded, 9; distressed New England troops, 19 –total 93.
Brunswick: Sick, 56 –total 56.
Amount of the whole, 338.

The number of sick and wounded…three hundred and thirty-eight; four-fifths…will soon join their …companies. I have not yet taken charge of near two thousand that are scattered up and down the country in cold barns, and who suffer exceedingly for want of comfortable apartments…. [388]

The loss of approximately 2300 soldiers due to illness and injury seriously hampered American efforts to maintain an effective fighting force. Those needing medical care also placed an additional strain placed upon ever more scarce resources. The state of the art of medicine at the time did little to alleviate the burdens of the ill and wounded. Infighting and disorganization among the physicians seriously hampered the provision of adequate care to the patients. Colonel William Smallwood of Maryland best describes the general impressions of the medical services held by the officers and soldiers at the time. In a letter to the Maryland Council of Safety written in October 1776 he relates "Our next greatest suffering proceeds from the great neglect of the sick; …there is not only a shameful but even an inhuman neglect daily exhibited. The Directors of the General Hospital…are extremely remiss and inattentive to the well-being and comfort of these unhappy men; I have withdrawn all of mine long ago and placed them in …a house in the country…. I foresee the evils arising from the shameful neglect…. [389] The story of the Continental Army medical service, its trials and failures, is to broad to be adequately represented in this manuscript. For further reading on the subject I refer to Mary C. Gillett's informative work on the subject. [390]

Call to Arms
The Flying Camp had evolved from its original concept as solely a mobile reserve, developing into a defensive force. It protected the approaches to the middle colonies and supplied troops for the main Army in New York. General Mercer being a man of action, chaffed under the reins applied by circumstance and decree. He wanted to

---

[387] Force, *Archives,* 5th Ser, Vol. 1. 346.
[388] Force, *Archives,* 5th Ser, Vol.3. 463.
[389] Force, *Archives,* 5th Ser, Vol.2. 1099-1100.
[390] For a further study on the Continental Army medical service I recommend Mary C. Gillett. *Army Historical Series,* "The Army Medical Department 1775-1818." Wash DC: Center of Military History US Army. 1981.

take the fight to the enemy. General Washington supported the idea and promoted efforts to utilize the Flying Camp in offensive actions. The "Partisan Party" raid against Staten Island on July 18th is one example.   Although an unfulfilled goal it was not the sole effort by General Mercer to use his command offensively.

The General had hoped to engage the enemy from the first day he was appointed to the Flying Camp. On October 15th he was finally able to put his long cherished plan into action. He and his forces crossed to Staten Island. The plan of assault was to march to the east end of the Island by daybreak where it was intended to attack the British. Initially, he had been joined by General Nathanael Greene and his command. At eleven o'clock that night orders were received from General Washington necessitating General Greene's return to Harlem. General Mercer's remaining force then consisted of New Jersey Militia from the Blazing Star post, Elizabethtown, and Newark. The Americans advanced towards the town of Richmond. Information was received indicating "that a company of *British* troops, one of *Hessians* and one of *Skinner's* Militia, lay there." The first objective of the raid then became the reduction of that post. [391]

The assault and exchange of fire was brief. Most of the enemy fled after exchanging a few shots. The Americans killed two and took seventeen prisoners. Two Americans were killed in the action and two senior officers were wounded. The list of prisoners included nine British troops and eight Hessians. The "Arms and Accoutrements" captured included eleven muskets, nine bayonets, five scabbards, ten cartridge-boxes, three cutlasses, three slings, one sword belt, 68 musket-balls, and 30 cartridges.[392] General Mercer's move against Staten Island was cut short by orders directing his return to New Jersey. A disappointed Mercer conceded that surprise and momentum had been lost. Writing to John Hancock afterwards he says: "Any further operations against the enemy would, however, have been, at that time, unsuccessful, as they were fully apprised of our approach, and had time sufficient to retire within their redoubts, and under cover of the ships at the watering-place." [393] The General wasn't a man prone to making excuses or complaining about failures. His movements and actions had been closely watched by spies and duly reported to the enemy. His skirmish at Richmond turned out to be with an outpost that was preparing to withdraw. The main portion of the enemy had departed earlier, which surely disappointed this aggressive commander. [394]

---

[391] ibid. 1093.
[392] Ibid. 1093-1094.
[393] Ibid. 1093.
[394] Waterman. 130.

An interesting side light to this action is the interrogation of one of the prisoners taken at Richmond. Private Christian Guiler was among the eight "Hessians" captured. His remarks vividly illustrate the plight of many of the German troops shipped to America. Private Guiler's examination took place on October 16th, at the Headquarters at Perth Amboy. The record states:

> [He] Says, tis eight years since he left his own country; almost all these troops are with General *Howe;* twelve thousand of them have come; expect more; expected if taken prisoner, to have mercy shown him if we were a Christian people; that he was brought from his country by force; that detachments were sent through their country, and if their parents interfered, were put in jail; were told they were to be garrisoned in *England*, but after three days arrival in *England*, were ordered to embark for *America,* to their great disapointment and against their will; were guarded to their ships; they saw no papers of any kind among them from us; if they knew they would be well treated by us, would all lay down their arms; have no desire to return to their regiment again; are much pleased and happy with the treatment that they have received, and are very thankful for the same." [395]

Private Guiler's comments reflect the forced servitude imposed upon many of the German troops raised for service with the British. The interrogation appears cordial as the soldier volunteered many details about his unit. The morale, and impressions held, among the Germans regarding their service and the enemy are well represented. When General Washington became aware of the eight German prisoners he suggested some be allowed to escape. It was hoped they would return to their units with tales of kind treatment and advertisements of Congress which may induce mutiny or desertions. [396]

A Not So Grand Finale

General Mercer's offensives were little more than annoying raids to the British Army. The British advances upon Forts Washington and Lee constituted the beginning of the campaign across New Jersey. From that point until the Battle of Trenton General Mercer and the remnants of the Flying Camp would be on the defensive and in retreat.

---

[395] Force, *Archives,* 5th Ser, Vol. 2. 1073-1074.
[396] Waterman. 131.

The end of the service commitment for the troops of the Flying Camp was quickly approaching. The original December 1st date of discharge as established by Congress was fast approaching. No effort to reestablish the Camp appears. Military defeats, the forced retreat, and the inability to raise and retain adequate numbers of troops combined to make the concept unsupportable. The decision of Congress to establish a national army eclipsed the need and role for the unit. The loss of the Flying Camp troops could not have come at a worse possible time for General Washington. Writing to the Congress on November 23rd, he pressed for troops and for money to pay the few remaining Flying Camp members, as a hopeful inducement towards retaining their services:

> I have not yet heard that any provision is making to supply the place of the troops composing the Flying Camp, whose departure is now at hand. The situation of our affairs is truly critical and such as requires uncommon exertions …. From the movements of the enemy …, they certainly will make a push to possess themselves …of the Jerseys. In order that you may be fully appraised of our weakness and of the necessity there is of our obtaining early succor, I have …directed General Mifflin to wait on you. He is intimately acquainted with our circumstances and will represent them better than my hurried state will allow…. Before I conclude, I would mention if an early and immediate supply of money could be sent…to pay the flying camp troops, it might have a happy effect. They would subsist themselves comfortably on their return-provide many necessaries of which they are in great want, …it might be the means of inducing many after seeing their friends to engage again. I expected on coming here to have met with many of the militia, but find from inquiry…. No more than four to five hundred at different posts. [397]

The General provided a report of the strength of the Army then with him at Newark (see table 6).

General Steven's Brigade	600
General Beall's (term expire 1st December)	1200
General Heard's(same)	800
Colonel Hand's	600
Colonel Smallwood's Regiment	200
Colonel Durkee's (time expire 1st January)	250
Colonel Hutchinson's (time expire 1st January)	100
Colonel Bradly's (time expire 1st December)	60
General Ewing's (time expire 1st January)	600
Lord Stirling's	1000 Total 5,410

Table 6: *Abstract of the Return of the Troops now at and near New-Ark fit for duty.* [398] (dated November 23rd, 1776).

---

[397] Force, *Archives,* 5th Ser, Vol. 3. 821.
[398] Ibid. 822.

Writing to John Hancock on November 30th the General relates that the turnout of New Jersey militia forces was limited. He notes that "Added to this, I have no assurances that more than a very few of the troops composing the Flying Camp will remain after the time of their engagement is out. He continues "…some of General Ewing's brigade, who stand engaged to the 1st of January, are now going away. If those go whose service expires this day, our force will be reduced to a mere handful." [399] Writing to General William Heath on December 12th, General Washington relates that "our situation at present in this quarter is truly critical. Our Army … has been greatly diminished. The troops composing the Flying Camp have mostly gone home…."[400] He reports further, "My numbers were now reduced to three thousand men."[401]

In lieu of additional forces, and with the disintegration of the Flying Camp, he was not going to allow one of his best generals to be stranded without a command. He formed a new brigade for General Mercer. It consisted of the remains of Smallwood's Maryland Regiment, Weber's Pennsylvania Corps, Haslet's Delaware Regiment, the 3rd Regiment of Virginia, and Durkee's Regiment of Connecticut. Although a small unit in numbers it was a highly experienced group of fine quality. The Third Virginia, commanded by his brother-in-law Colonel Weedon, was Mercer's old command, and welcomed. The others were men he had served with and commanded and were his friends; a suitable gathering of patriots amid a period of threatened disaster. [402]

The American retreat across New Jersey is sometimes portrayed as a rout of dismal and dejected soldiers, unwilling to fight a superior enemy. Closer examination reveals the British didn't enjoy an easy trek in their advance. In his retirement across the region General Washington left behind a trail, broken and impeded. Upon which the British were forced to give chase; forcing a three week march for them to move seventy miles in level country. A British account of their advance is revealing of the true course they had to follow and the obstacles faced:

> Jersey is a beautiful, though mostly flat country, but there are numerous small woods and dense thickets. In one of these woods several of our scouts were killed. They were supposed to have scouted to the front and sides, but they had not done so efficiently enough. They were suddenly surrounded, and so were lost. Following this incident the troop of 150 rebels hastily retired, without our being able to chastise them. [403]

As the British advanced towards Trenton they had to deal with American forces operating on their flanks. Captain Frederich von Muenchhausen reflects in his accounts that "General Lee, who is in our rear, makes our support line very unsafe. He often sends out raiding parties. Last night one of them captured a small escort with eight baggage wagons." The Captain notes later that public notice was given that:

> inhabitants who ventured, in mobs or individually, to fire at our passing men, would be hanged at the next tree without trial. It is very unsafe for us to travel in Jersey. The rascal peasants meet our men alone or in small unarmed groups. They have their rifles hidden in the bushes, or

[399] Ibid.919.
[400] Ibid. 1185.
[401] Ibid. 1186.
[402] Waterman.137.
[403] von Muenchhausen. 6

ditches, and the like. When they believe they are sure of success and they see one or several men belonging to our army, they shoot them in the head, then quickly hide their rifles and pretend they know nothing.[404]

At Trenton General Howe found the Americans had retreated across the river. General Washington had ordered all boats along the New Jersey shore of the river removed. Captain Von Muenchhausen reflects that "It is a great pity that we cannot get across the Delaware River. If we could, nothing would stand in the way of our getting to Philadelphia before the year is out." He mentions that Hessian troops were sent along the "Delaware River toward Philadelphia to look for boats or to find any other means of crossing this cursed river. "[405] The British advance had reached its high tide mark in the march across New Jersey. And the tide would recede with the American attacks upon Trenton and Princeton.

Crossing the Delaware. Painting by Emanuel Leutze. 66-G-15D-25.[406]

On Christmas Day, Hugh Mercer and some of the last remnants of the defunct Flying Camp accompanied General Washington in crossing the ice filled Delaware River. They were assigned to the force approaching Trenton from the north. General Greene was in overall command of this column, which General Washington accompanied. The assault was rapid; the Hessians turned out quickly and counterattacked the Americans approaching from the north. Their columns though were broken by the American's artillery and fire from General Mercer's troops flanking from the west. The German's then surrendered in fairly rapid fashion. General Washington's December 26th "Return of Prisoners" captured reflects a total of 918 troops taken, the capture of six three-pounder

[404] Ibid. 7
[405] Ibid. 7
[406] Pictures of the Revolutionary War. http://www.archives.gov/research/american-revolution/pictures/images/revolutionary-war-031.jpg, August 25th 2005.

guns and three ammunition wagons and many accoutrements. [407] Conditions did not support a continuation of the advance, forcing the Americans to retire across the Delaware. From the British viewpoint, Captain Von Muenchhausen reflected afterwards that for the Hessian commander at Trenton, "to his good fortune, Colonel Rall died the same day from his wounds; I say this because he would have lost his head if he had lived. This unhappy occurrence has caused us to leave the whole of Jersey except for posts at Brunswick and Amboy."[408]

General Washington elected to again cross the Delaware on December 30th, in an effort to launch a spoiling attack and prevent the British from crossing the river. Confronted by General Cornwallis near Trenton on January 1st, he conducted a masterful night withdrawal; leaving his campfires burning. Moving his forces towards Princeton he executed "a brilliant strategic envelopment" that led to the Battle of Princeton on January 3rd. [409]

Exodus

By then, General Mercer's brigade had been seriously depleted, consisting of only 400 men. It was with a collection of such small forces that General Washington planned to flank the main British force and attack its rear guard. General Mercer's Brigade was in the advance guard which departed the camp at one o'clock (AM). He intended to secure the bridge at Stony Brook, to prevent reinforcements from reaching Princeton or the escape of British troops out of the town. The American's approaching Stony Brook encountered the British 17th Infantry Regiment. After firing three vollies the British advanced with bayonets upon the American line. The fear among Mercer's men of facing the dreaded British bayonet caused them to break rank and run. Riding his horse into the front of his troops to rally them it was shot and he fell. Some of the British troops quickly surrounded him. Seeing his rank they shouted "The rebel General is captured." Surrounded by bayonets Mercer was called upon to surrender. He instead lunged with his sword at his enemy and was impaled by bayonets; receiving seventeen wounds and being left for dead upon the field.

General Washington's arrival with reinforcements rallied the troops, turning them upon the British and forcing a retreat. Major John Armstrong, Mercer's aide, found his commander alive but unconscious. He was taken to the farmhouse of a local Quaker family for treatment. The British captured the house, taking General Mercer prisoner. He would linger on death's door for nearly two weeks. General Washington would say of the Battle of Princeton that his successes there were "countered balanced by the death of the brave and worthy General Mercer." The American losses included many former Flying Camp members : General Mercer, Colonel Haslet, and others.[410]

---

[407] Force, *Archives,* 5th Ser, Vol. 3. 1444-1445.
[408] von Muenchhausen. 9.
[409] Boatner. 786.
[410] Waterman. 110.

Washington at Princeton, Jan. 3, 1777. Lithograph by D. McLellan, 1853. 148-GW-331[411]

Glory denied, sacrifice forgotten

The Flying Camp was envisioned and effectively served as a deterrent against a British invasion of the middle colonies. It is reasonable to conclude that the presence of General Mercer's force in New Jersey impacted General Howe's offensive plans. The British Army and Navy could have assaulted any location in the region with over powering force and certain victory. An attack by General Howe realized upon New Jersey would have seriously expose his right flank to the American Army in New York. An advance upon Philadelphia, the obvious prize, would have resulted in the British Army being cut off from its base by Washington's Army approaching from behind. General Howe would have lost his line of supply, his naval support, and his only line of retreat. It was necessary for him to first deal with Washington's forces in New York. Then he could advance on a single front into New Jersey. This he did with the onslaught against Long Island and his advance against New York. Howe would still face Washington in New Jersey. But he faced a single, now decimated army offering far less of a challenge to his advance.

The effort to raise the 10,000 men desired for the Flying Camp fell far short of its goal. The Camp was slow to be organized and was never completely formed. The quality of the troops raised was generally poor. Desertions were a serious challenge to Generals Washington and Mercer in their efforts to establish a useful force. Problems involving communications, logistics, organization, and training were difficult to manage

---

[411] Pictures of the Revolutionary War. http://www.archives.gov/research/american-revolution/pictures/index.html#1776. August 19, 2005.

and were seldom overcome. Localism and rivalry between the States played negative roles in the staffing and manning of the unit. The intent of providing "a pool of men or units, which would serve as a reserve force for emergencies for the Continental Army," was essentially not achieved.[412] The quotas had to be met through the use of existing forces. The units raised were quickly needed on the front and unavailable to constitute a reserve force. The sustained efforts of a relatively few individuals were the driving force behind even the lackluster success that was achieved.

The efforts expended in creating and developing the Flying Camp failed in providing sufficient numbers of capable soldiers for the American Army. This failure was the catalyst for the change needed in the way the Americans would raise and field a competent army. As a deterrent aligned against General Howe's forces on Staten Island it can be considered a success. The British deferred from attacking directly into the middle colonies. Instead they marched against General Washington's main Army, moving against New York first.

The Flying Camp can be regarded either as a noble experiment and gallant effort; or as a lackluster success and failed enterprise. It must reasonably be seen as a failure in its intended goals. Still, the experiment served to test the Americans ability to mobilize and field an effective military force. It provided the forge necessary for casting the metal needed to form a stronger national army. It stands as an example of the desire and effort expended by our founding Father's (and mother's, as Abigail Adams would remind us) to deal with the events encountered. Few singular efforts in the history of humankind stand alone as unqualified successes. Most are the results of trial and error, failure upon failure, until success is eventually achieved. So it is with the events surrounding the American Revolutionary War. A series of failures compounded over a period of nearly a decade and culminating in success. The Flying Camp was one effort, reasonably judged a failure yet part of the final success.

While researching this story I've come to realize that it represents an unfinished epic. I cannot come to the point of saying "The End." The circumstances and events occurring in the America of 1776 are striking similar to those faced by the many people in the world today. "History is a story, the greatest story," and it is a never ending story, often repeated with minor variations, and many similarities. The Story Continues.

---

[412] Newland, 141.

Appendix

...the world...A stage where every man must play a part.
(William Shakespeare; *Merchant of Venice, Act 1, Scene 1.*)

The major and minor roles played by many different actors involved with the Flying Camp are highly worthy of mention. The roles of some individuals have been presented here in detail, while others will remain unknown and unsung. All are appreciated, some in absentia from the pages of history, others abundantly recognized by grateful generations of free Americans. The following is a list of prominent players: staff, officers, and others associated with the Camp. With some exceptions, the majority of this list comes from the excellent work of William H. Richardson. [327]

...Luminaries

Lieutenant General George Washington: Commander-In-Chief.
Brigadier General Hugh Mercer: Commander of the Flying Camp.
Brigadier General Daniel Roberdeau – Pennsylvania
Brigadier General James Ewing – Pennsylvania
Brigadier General Rezin Beall – Maryland
Colonel Clement Biddle, Deputy Quarter Master General
Gustavius Resberg, Assistant Deputy Quarter Master General
Johnathan B. Smith, Deputy Muster Master General (Resigned September 25th, 1776)*
William Davis, Deputy Muster Master General (Appointed October 7th, 1776)*
Benjamin Flower, Commissary Military Stores
Lieutenant (Lt.) Colonel Monsieur Jacques Antoine de Franchessian, Engineer
Lt. Colonel Monsieur Kirmovan, Engineer
Captain Samuel Davis, Assistant Engineer
Richard Dallam, Deputy Paymaster General
Samuel Griffith, Deputy Adjutant General
Dr. William Shippen, Jr., Chief Physician
Dr. William Brown, Assistant Physician (Appointed September 24th, 1776)*
* Details extracted from Force, *Archives, 5th Ser, Vol. 2.*

...Regimental Commanders and Officers...
....New Jersey

Colonels: Theunis Dey, Daniel Hendrickson, William Maxwell, George Taylor, Mark Thompson, Whitton Cripps, Jacob Ford, Daniel Forman, Charles Read, and Edward Thomas.
Lt. Colonels and Majors: Abraham Bonnell, Ellis Cook, John Dunn, John Duychink, William Ellis, John Maur. Goetschius, Samuel Haynes, Josiah Hillman, and Enos Kelsey.

....Connecticut

Colonels: Philip Burr Bradley, and John Durkee.
Lt. Colonels: William Shepard, and Thomas Knowlton.

....*Delaware*

Colonels: Thomas McKean, John Haslet, and Samuel Patterson.
Lt. Colonels: Gunning Bedford, George Latimer.
Majors: John McPhearson (killed in Quebec), Thomas McDonough.
Captains: William Moody, Joseph Caldwell, Thomas Kean, James Dunn,
Thomas Skillington, Matt Manlove, John Woodgate, Nathaniel Mitchell.
Surgeon James Tilton, and Chaplain Joseph Montgomery.[413]

.... *Maryland*

Colonels: Thomas Ewing, Charles Greenbury Griffith,
Josias Carvil Hall, Henry Hellingsworth, William Richardson, and William
Smallwood.
Major: Mordecai Gist.
Captains: Jacob Good, James Hindman, Solomon Long, Peter Mantz,
John Allen Thomas, Edward Veazey (Veazy), John Gunby, John Watkins
Thomas Woolford.

.... *Pennsylvania*

Colonels: Samuel John Atlee, William Baxter, James Cunningham,
_____ Dill, Curtis Grub, _____Guyger, Henry Haller, Joseph Hart,
David Kennedy, Peter Kichline (Kichlein) , Samuel Mifflin, Richard
McCallister, Samuel Miles, William Montgomery, George Ross, Matthias
Swope, Frederick Watts, [414]_____ Allison, _____ Henderson, _____
Klotz, _____Moore, ___Savitz, _____Slough.
Lt. Colonels and Majors: Thomas Bell, _____ Burd, _____ Lawrence,
Nicholas Lutz, James Moore, _____ Parry, _____ Tea. [415] Captain
Benjamin Loxley, Captain-Lieutenant Benjamin Armitage, First
Lieutenant Francis Price (Grice), Second Lieutenant James Nevill[416]

---

413 Whiteley. 11, 20. source for Delaware starting with Latimer.
414 Richardson. 160-161.
415 *PA Archives* ...'War of the Revolution", 761-763.
416 Loxley, Muster roll.

Bibliography

Unpublished Primary Sources:

Armstrong, William. *Orderly Book 1776, 1778-1779*. Historical Society of Pennsylvania, Philadelphia, PA.

Loxley, Benjamin. *A Journal of the Campaign to Amboy of the Parts of Jersey, 1776*. Historical Society of Pennsylvania, Philadelphia, PA.

Published Primary Sources:

Adlum, John. *Memoirs of the Life of John Adlum in the Revolutionary War*. Ed. Howard H. Peckham. Chicago: Caxton Club, 1968.

Force, Peter, ed. *American Archives*: Fourth Series, Volume VI. "A Documentary History of the English Colonies in North America from the King's Message to Parliament of March 7,1774 to the Declaration of Independence of the United States." Washington: M. St. Claire Clarke and Peter Force, 1846.

_____. *American Archives*: Fifth Series, Volumes I, 2, 3. "A Documentary History of the United States of America from the Declaration of Independence, July 4, 1776 to the Definitive Treaty of Peace with Great Britain, September 3, 1783." Washington: M. St Claire Clarke & Peter Force, 1848.

Graham, Michael. *The Revolution Remembered : Eyewitness Accounts of the War for Independence*. Ed. John C. Dann. Chicago: University of Chicago Press, 1980.

Greene, Nathanael. *The Papers of Nathanael Greene,* Chapel Hill NC: University of North Carolina Press, 1976.

Jefferson, Thomas. *The Papers of Thomas Jefferson, Volume 1, 1760 –1776*. Eds. Julian P Boyd, Lyman H Butterfield, and Mira R Bryan. Princeton: Princeton Univ. Press, 1950.

Journals of the House of Representatives of the Commonwealth of Pennsylvania. Vol.1. Philadelphia: John Dunlap, 1782.

Maryland Historical Society. *Archives of Maryland: Muster Rolls and Other Records of Service of Maryland Troops in the American Revolution 1775-1783*. Baltimore: Maryland Historical Society, 1900.

Muenchhausen, Captain Frederich von. *At General Howe's Side 1776-1778: the Diary of Howe's Aide de Camp*. Ernest Kipping and Samuel Smith translators. Monmouth Beach NJ: Philip Freneau Press, 1974.

Pennsylvania Archives. *Pennsylvania in the War of the Revolution, Associated Battalions and Militia 1775-1783*, William H Eggle, Ed. Harrisburg: E. K. Meyers, 1888.

Public Archives Commission. *Delaware Archives*. "Military." Wilmington DE: Mercantile, 1911, 1974r.

Smith, Paul H, Ed. *Letters of Delegates to Congress 1774-1789*. Washington: Library of Congress, 1979.

Washington, George. *The Writings of George Washington from the Original Manuscript Sources 1745-1799*. Ed. John C. Fitzpatrick. Wash DC: US Government Printing Office, 1932) .Vol. 5.

Secondary Sources:
Ballas, Henry Hobart. *A History of the Delaware State Society of the Cincinnati.* Wilmington DE: Historical Society of Delaware, 1895.

Berg, Fred A. *Encyclopedia of Continental Army Units: Battalions, Regiments and Independent Corps.* Harrisburg PA: Stackpole Books, 1972.

Boatner, Mark. *Encyclopedia of the American Revolution*, Mechanicsburg PA: Stackpole Books, 1994.

Carrington, Henry B. *Battles of the American Revolution 1775-1781.* New York: A S Barnes, 1876.

_____. *Battle Maps and Charts of the American Revolution with Explanatory Notes and School History References.* Chicago: A.S. Barnes,1881.

Chadwick, Bruce. *George Washington's War.* Naperville Illionis:Sourcebooks,2004.

Curtis, Edward E. *The Organization of the British Army in the American Revolution.* New Haven: Yale Univ. Press, 1926.

Deary, William Paul. *Toward Disaster at Fort Washington. November 1776.* Ann Arbor: UMI, 1995.

Fischer, David Hackett. *Washington's Crossing.* New York: Oxford University Press, 2004.

Freeman, Douglas Southall. *George Washington: a Biography.* "Leader of the Revolution." New York: Charles Scribner's Sons, 1948-57.

Ganoe, William Addleman, *The History of the United States Army.* New York: D Appleton, 1924.

Gillett, Mary C. *Army Historical Series,* "The Army Medical Department 1775-1818." Wash DC: Center of Military History US Army. 1981.

Huston, James A. *Army History Series:* "Sinews of War: Army Logistics 1775-1953." Washington DC: Office of the Chief of Military History. 1966.

Kail, Jerry. *Who Was Who During the American Revolution.* New York: Bobbs-Merrill Inc.1976.

Lefferts, Charles M. *Uniforms of the American, British, French and German Armies in the War of American Revolution 1775-1780.* Old Greenwich CT: WE, Inc. 1971.

Lundin, Leonard. *Cockpit of the Revolution, The War for Independence in New Jersey.* Princeton: Princeton University Press, 1940.
Meadows, Eric I. *The Battle of Long Island.* Monmouth Beach NJ: Frenew Press, 1978.

Middlekauff, Robert. *The Glorious Cause: The American Revolution 1763-1789.* C Van Woodward, Ed. New York: Oxford Univ. Press, 1982.

Minnis, M. Lee. *First Virginia Regiment of Foot 1775-1783.* Westminster MD: Willow Bend Books, 1998.

Newland, Samuel, *The Pennsylvania Militia: The Early Years 1669-1792.* Anneville, PA: Pennsylvania National Guard Association, 1997.

Ousterhout, Anne M. *A State Divided: Opposition in Pennsylvania to the American Revolution.* New York: Greenwood Press, 1987.

Pamphlets in American History, Group 1, (microform).Sanford, NC :Microfilming Corporation of America,1979.

Peden, Henry C. *Revolutionary Patriots of Frederick County, Maryland 1775-1783.* Westminster MD: Willow Bend Books, 2000.

_____. *Revolutionary Patriots of Worcester & Somerset Counties, Maryland 1775-1783.* Westminster MD: Willow Bend Books, 2000.

Pearson, Michael. *Those Damned Rebels: the American Revolution as Seen Through the Eyes of the British.* New York: G.P. Putnam's Sons, 1972.

Purcell, L. Edward. *Who Was Who in the American Revolution.* New York: Facts on File, 1993.

Robert B Roberts. *Encyclopedia of Historic Forts,* New York: MacMillan Publishing Company, 1988.

Sanborn, Paul J. "Flying Camp (July –November 1776)," *The American Revolution 1775-1783 : An Encyclopedia.* Blanco, Richard L Ed.,New York: Garland Publishing, 1993.

Scharf, J Thomas. *History of Maryland from the Earliest Period to the Present Day.* Baltimore: Piet, 1879.

Selby, John E. *The Revolution in Virginia 1775-1783.* Williamsburg VA: Colonial Williamsburg Foundation,1988.

Smith, George, *A Universal Military Dictionary.* Whitehall: J. Millan, 1779.

Smith, Samuel Stelle. *The Battle of Trenton.* Monmouth Beach, NJ: Philip Freneau Press, 1965.

Steuart, Rieman. *A History of the Maryland Line in the Revolutionary War,* Maryland: Society of the Cininnati of Maryland, 1969.

Stryker, William S. *The Battles of Trenton and Princeton.* Boston: Houghton, Mifflin and Co, The Riverside Press, 1898.

The National Cyclopedia of American Biography being the History of the United States as Illustrated in the lives of the founders, builders and defenders of the republic, and of the men and women who are doing the work, and molding the thought of the present time. New York: James T. White & Co. 1899.

Trussell, John B. B. Jr. Pennsylvania Historical and Museum Commission, *The Pennsylvania Line: Regimental Organization and Operations, 1776-1783 /.* Harrisburg: The Commission, 1977.

Ward, Christopher L. *The Delaware Continentals 1776-1786.* Willington DE: Historical Society of Delaware, 1941.

Waterman, Joseph M.. *With Sword and Lancet: The Life of General Hugh Mercer.* Richmond VA: Garrett & Massie.1941.

Whiteley, William G. *The Revolutionary Soldiers of Delaware.* Wilmington DE: James & Webb, 1875.

Wright, Robert K., Jr. *Army Lineage Series.* "The Continental Army." Washington DC: US Army, 1983.

Electronic Sources:

Bland, James. *Carry Me Back to Old Virginny,*(1878). www. netstate.com/state/symb/song/va-carry-me-back

Connecticut Society of the Sons of the American Revolution. *LT. COL.Thomas Knowlton: Connecticut's Forgotten Hero.*[electronic edition]. [Online]: http://www.ctssar.org. October 2004.

Continental Congress of the United States, 2nd Session. *A Century of Lawmaking for a New Nation.* United States Congressional Documents, Journals of the Continental Congress, Volume 5. HTTP:// [Online]:http://memory.loc.gov/ll/lljc/005/0100/0100565.gif.

Hynson George B, William S. Brown. *Official State Songs: Delaware State Song.* (1925) www. netstate.com/state/symb/song/de-song.

Khoury Eddie, Ronnie Banner. *Pennsylvania.*(1989) www.netstate.com/state/symb/song/pa-pa.

Library of Congress, The American Revolution and Its Era: Maps and Charts of North America and the West Indies,1750-1789.[Online] Available http://memory.loc.gov/, Library of Congress, Washington DC. 6/6/05.

Maryland State Archives. *Archives of Maryland (Biographical Series)* "Thomas Johnson 1732-1819". Maryland State Archives, Annapolis:[Online]:www.mdarchives.state.md.us

Maryland State Archives. *Archives of Maryland Online: Journals and Correspondence of the Maryland Council of Safety, July 7: December 31, 1776,* Vol12, Maryland State Archives, Annapolis:[Online]: www.aomol.net/html/index.html .

Maryland State Archives. *Archives of Maryland Online: Proceedings of the Conventions of the Province of Maryland, 1774-1776,* Vol 78. Maryland State Archives, Annapolis:[Online]:www.mdarchives.state.md.us .

Maryland State Archives. *Archives of Maryland Online,, Muster Rolls and Other Records of Service of Maryland Troops in the American Revolution 1775-1783,* Vol 18. Maryland State Archives, Annapolis:[Online]:www.mdarchives.state.md.us...

Massachusetts Historical Society. *Adams Family Papers: An Electronic Archive..* [Online]: www.masshist.org/digitaladams/ .

Ralph, Stanley L. *Nutmeg* (State Cantata), (2003) ,www. netstate.com/state/symb/song/ct-the nutmeg

National Archives and Records Administration. Pictures of the Revolutionary War. Select Audiovisual Records. National Archives and Records Administration, Washington, DC 20408. http://www.archives.gov/research/american-revolution/pictures/index.html#1776. Randall, James Ryder. *Maryland , My Maryland.* (April 1861). www. netstate.com/state/symb/song/md-my-md.

Washington, George. "The Diaries of George Washington". Vol 3. Donald Jackson, ed.; Dorothy Twohig, assoc. ed. "The Papers of George Washington." Charlottesville: University Press of Virginia, 1978.*" The George Washington Papers at the Library of Congress, 1741-1799.* John C. Fitzpatrick, Ed. [Online]:www.memory.loc.gov.

Washington, George. "The Writings of George Washington from the Original Manuscript Sources 1745-1799.*" The George Washington Papers at the Library of Congress, 1741-1799.* John C. Fitzpatrick, Ed. [Online]:www.memory.loc.gov.

Periodical Sources:
Benson, Evelyn Abraham. "Identification of Lt. Thomas Wynne of the Flying Camp, 1776" *Pennsylvania Genealogical Magazine,* Vol. 29, no.2, 1975.

Devine, Francis E. "The Pennsylvania Flying Camp, July-November 1776". *Pennsylvania History.* (January 1979) Vol.4.

Richardson, William H. "Washington and the New Jersey Campaign of 1776." *Proceedings of the New Jersey Historical Society.* (April 1932), Vol. 50.no 2.

Index

CPSIA information can be obtained
at www.ICGtesting.com
Printed in the USA
LVOW09s1947250617

539313LV00031BA/1004/P

9 780806 355061